Peaceful

Meditations

for
Every Day in
Ordinary Time

—❦—

Weeks 1–9

YEARS A, B, & C

Peaceful

Meditations

for
Every Day in
Ordinary Time

—⚜—

Weeks 1–9

Rev. Warren J. Savage
Mary Ann McSweeny

Liguori
ONE LIGUORI DRIVE
LIGUORI MO 63057-9999

Imprimi Potest:
Harry Grile, CSsR, Provincial
Denver Province, The Redemptorists

Published by Liguori Publications
Liguori, Missouri 63057

To order, call 800–325–9521
www.liguori.org

Copyright © 2012 Warren J. Savage and Mary Ann McSweeny

Library of Congress Cataloging–in–Publication Data
Library of Congress Cataloging-in-Publication Data

Savage, Warren J.
  Peaceful meditations for every day of ordinary time : weeks 1/9, cycles
A, B, and C / Warren J. Savage and Mary Ann McSweeny. — 1st ed.
    p. cm.
  ISBN 978-0-7648-2142-4
  1. Church year—Prayers and devotions. 2. Catholic Church—Prayers
and devotions. 3. Catholic Church. Lectionary for Mass (U.S.) I.
McSweeny, Mary Ann. II. Title.
  BX2170.C55S35 2012
  242'.38—dc23

                                                              2012014671

Liguori Publications, a nonprofit corporation, is an apostolate of
The Redemptorists. To learn more about The Redemptorists, visit
Redemptorists.com.

Printed in the United States of America
16 15 14 13 12 / 5 4 3 2 1
First Edition

Contents

Introduction

Peace, a gift from God, is the core of our being. In our deepest heart space reside tranquillity, serenity, harmony, and complete trust in God's love for us.

In our busy lives, peace may seem to elude us. We may feel frantic with the number of tasks and obligations we face, overwhelmed with responsibilities, discouraged at how quickly time goes by and at how much we are forced to leave undone.

Yet if we take just a moment to consider what is really important in our lives, we become aware of a point of stillness in our being. That stillness is the voice of God calling us to let go of worry, anxiety, and distraction. It is the voice of God inviting us to spend time in quiet prayer, reading sacred Scripture, and meditating on how we can become more like Jesus in our everyday encounters. It is the voice of God asking us to be intentional about carrying the message of love, compassion, and peace to our families, friends, coworkers, and communities.

This book of meditations offers readers an opportunity to begin a daily ritual of reading and reflecting on sacred Scripture. It provides examples of the ordinary and extraordinary challenges life can bring and shows how the intentional imitation of Jesus can help us meet these challenges. It encourages the custom of daily prayer and suggests concrete practices to broaden our awareness of the presence of God in all people and to reach out in peace to help those in need. We have been honored with the gift of God's peace in our hearts. We are called to cultivate that gift, embody it, and give witness to it so that others come to understand more deeply the presence of God in and around us. Each day we can practice being a peacemaker. Each day we can lessen our anxiety and increase our peace with God. Each day we can be a messenger of God's peace, love, and compassion in this fragile world.

Weeks 1-9

The Baptism of the Lord
First Sunday in Ordinary Time

YEAR A

Isaiah 42:1–4, 6–7
Psalm 29:1–2, 3–4, 3, 9–10
Acts of the Apostles 10:34–38
Matthew 3:13–17

And when Jesus had been baptized, just as he came up from the water, suddenly the heavens were opened to him and he saw the Spirit of God descending like a dove and alighting on him. And a voice from heaven said, "This is my Son, the Beloved, with whom I am well pleased."

MATTHEW 3:16–17

Reflection: How often do we reflect on the meaning and significance of our baptism? To understand our baptism is to understand who we are and what our mission is in life. Baptism makes each of us a beloved son or daughter of the Triune God. Through baptism we become sisters and brothers with people from various cultures, nationalities, social backgrounds, languages, and ways of life. As children of God's family we share a common dignity, a common love, and a common vocation to be servants of God in the world. Baptism obliges us to be mindful of our communion with God and others and to live a life that promotes compassion, love, peace, unity, and the dignity of all people.

Perhaps one of the greatest challenges of the Christian spiritual life is to live with baptismal awareness that our true life is with God. Such awareness will prompt us to listen to the voice of God in the Scriptures, to make time for prayer, and to show compassion to the poor. Through baptism, we enter into a sacred mystery and are empowered by the Holy Spirit to share the inner life of the Triune God, who is love. God is pleased with us when we share the gift of unconditional love with all people, bringing about peace and unity.

Ponder: Is God pleased with me and the way I'm living at the moment?

Prayer: Lord, unblock the ears of my heart that I may hear your comforting voice of love, compassion, and peace.

Practice: Today I will live with baptismal awareness and recognize the dignity of all people.

YEAR B

Isaiah 42:1–4, 6–7 or Isaiah 55:1–11
Psalm 29:1–2, 3–4, 3, 9–10 or Isaiah 12:2–3, 4bcd, 5–6
Acts of the Apostles 10:34–38 or 1 John 5:1–9
Mark 1:7–11

For as the rain and the snow come down from heaven, and do not return there until they have watered the earth, making it bring forth and sprout, giving seed to the sower and bread to the eater, so shall my word be that goes out from my mouth; it shall not return to me empty, but it shall accomplish that which I purpose, and succeed in the thing for which I sent it.

ISAIAH 55:10–11

Reflection: At some unexpected moment along life's journey, we awaken to a voice deep inside our hearts that asks us, "What is the meaning and purpose in life?" For Christians, the meaning and purpose of life is revealed in Christ. Christ came into the world to bring all people into communion with God. His work on Earth was to share God's love and compassion with the hungry, the poor, the alienated, and the forgotten.

At baptism, we were incorporated into the body of Christ, the Church. As members of the body of Christ, we share in Jesus' mission of peace and reconciliation. Our lives must be interpreted in light of the life and ministry of Jesus.

Our baptism sets us apart to carry on the work of Christ, to spread the Word of God, to comfort the afflicted, and to be God's messengers of peace and unity in broken and fragile environments. As coworkers with Christ, we must use our gifts and talents for the common good and help bring forth in our world a community wherein all people are loved and respected as children of God. Baptism reminds us that our purpose in life is to be the seed of God's peace and the bread of God's compassion to humanity.

Ponder: What is God's will for me?

Prayer: Lord, help me to discern my gifts and talents and use them for the common good of all people.

Practice: Today I will actively promote peace and unity.

YEAR C

Isaiah 42:1–4, 6–7 or Isaiah 40:1–5, 9–11
Psalm 29:1–2, 3–4, 3, 9–10 or
Psalm 104:1b–2, 3–4, 24–25, 27–28, 29–30
Acts of the Apostles 10:34–38 or Titus 2:11–14; 3:4–7
Luke 3:15–16, 21–22

He will feed his flock like a shepherd; he will gather the lambs in his arms, and carry them in his bosom, and gently lead the mother sheep.

ISAIAH 40:11

Reflection: Baptism unites people from all nations into God's flock. In this flock many suffering children need our immediate attention and care. We learn about these children—many of whom are close to death—in newspapers and magazines and on TV documentaries.

In Africa, where there is widespread famine and drought, little children cry out for food and drink. In Haiti, where there is widespread HIV/AIDS, orphaned babies are desperate for medical resources. In the Middle East, where conflict and violence coexist, frightened, displaced children search for safety, security, and peace. In the United States, where everyone has the right to a good education, poor, illiterate children want to learn to read and succeed in life.

All over the world, there are motherless and fatherless children; homeless and abandoned children; children dying of famine, disease, violence, and war. These vulnerable children are God's lambs in need of a shepherd's care. They need committed, compassionate persons to feed them, to gather them, to carry them, and to lead them to a place of safety, security, and peace.

In baptism, we are configured to Christ, the Good Shepherd. Our baptism makes each of us God's instruments of compassion, love, and peace. The Spirit of God empowers us to use the gifts God has given us to work for justice, to help rebuild broken lives, and to offer people hope.

Ponder: Who in my life needs a shepherd's care?

Prayer: Lord, give me a shepherd's heart so that I can show your love and compassion to someone in need.

Practice: Today I will make others aware of the plight of children living in poverty and make a commitment to eradicate global poverty.

Monday of the
First Week in Ordinary Time

YEAR I
Hebrews 1:1–6
Psalm 97:1 and 2b, 6 and 7c, 9

YEAR II
1 Samuel 1:1–8
Psalm 116:12–13, 14–17, 18–19

YEARS I AND II
Mark 1:14–20

And Jesus said to them, "Follow me and I will make you fish for people." And immediately they left their nets and followed him.

MARK 1:17–18

Reflection: Jesus called ordinary fishermen to join him in the work of God. Jesus invited these ordinary people to join him in proclaiming the Gospel to others. This same invitation is extended to each of us and to people from various situations and cultures all over the world.

Letting go of their nets, leaving their boats behind, and turning their backs on the things they loved signaled the end of a successful fishing career and the beginning of a radically different calling. Their encounter with Jesus was a life-changing experience, one that caused them to reexamine every aspect of their lives and ultimately decide to risk everything to follow the call.

It's difficult to hear the voice of God and to respond to the invitation to follow Jesus amid the worldly chatter. Following Jesus in our hyperactive, hyperconnected society is a challenge. We are surrounded daily by many distractions, many forces competing for our attention, our hearts, our souls, and our bodies. We are afraid to let go of the things that make us secure and bring us temporary relief from life's daily struggles.

Finding time in our busy lives to read and meditate on the Word of God opens the way for us to follow and give witness to Jesus in the flow of life. When we read and meditate on the gospels, we encounter the same Jesus who changed the hearts of fishermen and called them to fish for people.

Ponder: What am I clinging to for security?

Prayer: Lord, give me the courage and strength to follow your call so that I may be a witness of love, compassion, and peace to others.

Practice: Today I will take inventory of my material possessions and give what I don't need to the poor.

Tuesday of the First Week in Ordinary Time

YEAR I
Hebrews 2:5–12
Psalm 8:2ab and 5, 6–7, 8–9

YEAR II
1 Samuel 1:9–20
1 Samuel 2:1, 4–5, 6–7, 8abcd

YEARS I AND II
Mark 1:21–28

They went to Capernaum; and when the sabbath came, [Jesus] entered the synagogue and taught. They were astounded at his teaching, for he taught them as one having authority, and not as the scribes.

MARK 1:21–22

Reflection: Jesus astounds us with the simplicity of his teaching: Love God and our neighbor as ourselves. He teaches us to live with God's law of love as our authority. He shows us how to love by teaching us compassion and forgiveness, faith and hope, patience and acceptance, justice and courage.

We, too, are teachers of one another. Our daily actions, words, and behaviors have the power to influence all those we meet. We teach compassion by being present to those who are ill or troubled. We teach forgiveness by letting go of hurts and resentments. We teach faith by relying on God to show us what to do. We teach hope by looking for the positive in our lives. We teach patience by practicing self-control and letting go of self-centeredness. We teach acceptance by trusting we are where we are supposed to be and enjoying the moment. We teach justice by speaking out on behalf of those who suffer from others' prejudice, indifference, and lack of integrity. We teach courage by moving forward despite our fears.

Every day we have a new opportunity to accept God as our authority and put our hope and trust in the power of love. Every day we have the choice to let Jesus teach us the way of compassion and forgiveness. Every day we have a chance to astound those we meet by our willingness to teach and give witness to God's love and peace.

Ponder: What am I teaching others?

Prayer: Lord, you are my teacher. Grant me the humility to learn your way of love.

Practice: Today I will teach love by speaking kindly and respectfully to everyone I encounter.

Wednesday of the First Week in Ordinary Time

YEAR I
Hebrews 2:14–18
Psalm 105:1–2, 3–4, 6–7, 8–9

YEAR II
1 Samuel 3:1–10, 19–20
Psalm 40:2 and 5, 7–8a, 8b–9, 10

YEARS I AND II
Mark 1:29–39

[Jesus] answered, "Let us go on to the neighboring towns, so that I may proclaim the message there also; for that is what I came out to do."

MARK 1:38

Reflection: Jesus does not restrict his teaching of the message of God's love to a favored few. He moves beyond the limits of what is comfortable and familiar to offer healing and compassion to everyone he can reach.

As we work to teach the message of God's love, we may find that we have limited our teaching to those we already love. We need to move beyond the familiar to face the challenge of loving those we don't know or who are difficult to love. We need to be consistent in our attitudes and words as we stretch beyond our comfort zones to live and breathe love into our troubled world.

To truly witness to God's love through our lives is a daily commitment. It takes awareness to accept the fear, arrogance, and indifference that prevent us from loving those we perceive as unworthy, untouchable, or undeserving. It takes courage to ask God to take away whatever blocks our ability to love unconditionally. It takes wisdom to discern the ways God calls us each day to move into new areas where we can bring the message of hope, peace, and love.

It is God's will that we love one another. We serve God best by humbly asking each day to be shown how to carry out God's will. God is our source of strength as we learn to walk the road of love wherever it may lead us, taking the risk to love beyond our self-imposed limits.

Ponder: Where do I bring the message of God's infinite love?

Prayer: Lord, you stoop toward me in love. Bless me with humility that I may let your law of love be written in my heart. Show me how to love my neighbor today.

Practice: Today I will go out of my way to help someone in need.

Thursday of the First Week in Ordinary Time

YEAR I
Hebrews 3:7–14
Psalm 95:6–7c, 8–9, 10–11

YEAR II
1 Samuel 4:1–11
Psalm 44:10–11, 14–15, 24–25

YEARS I AND II
Mark 1:40–45

Moved with pity, Jesus stretched out his hand and touched [the leper], and said to him, "I do choose. Be made clean!"

MARK 1:41

Reflection: Compassion dwells deep in our hearts. Our work is to open all our senses to feel its movement and obey its direction to reach out in love to others in need.

We need to listen to the movement of compassion when we hear of people whose lives are devastated by natural disasters. We need to let go of painful memories of war between our countries and let the compassion in our hearts lead us to help.

We need to listen to the movement of compassion when we hear of drought and famine in East Africa.

We need to let go of our indifference to people thousands of miles away who may not look, talk, or think like us but who need our support to survive.

We need to listen to the movement of compassion in our everyday lives when those who have hurt us ask our forgiveness. We need to be ready to let go of resentment and the desire to withhold our love and reach out in reconciliation.

We need to listen to the movement of compassion when we face how we have injured others. We need to take ownership of our actions and words and risk asking for forgiveness.

God's gift of compassion moves us to reach out to others in love and understanding of the reality of suffering. Walking with others in compassion, we bring a message of hope and healing to the world.

Ponder: When has compassion moved me to reach out to others?

Prayer: Lord, you are always reaching out in love to touch me. Open my eyes, ears, and heart to feel the movement of compassion in my heart. Let me be an instrument of your healing and forgiveness.

Practice: Today I will spend five minutes quietly listening to my heart.

Friday of the First Week in Ordinary Time

YEAR I
Hebrews 4:1–5, 11
Psalm 78:3 and 4bc, 6c–7, 8

YEAR II
1 Samuel 8:4–7, 10–22a
Psalm 89:16–17, 18–19

YEARS I AND II
Mark 2:1–12

So many gathered around that there was no longer room for them, not even in front of the door; and [Jesus] was speaking the word to them.

MARK 2:2

Reflection: We are all hungry for the Word of God—the word of love, peace, forgiveness, reconciliation, and hope. Yet when we think about the number of words we exchange in a day, how many of them truly reflect the Word of God? What if we deliberately chose only respectful, kind, and encouraging words to communicate with family, friends, colleagues, community members—and ourselves?

Instead of venting our frustrations on others, we could go for a walk and vent to God.

Instead of lying to cover up sneaky behavior, we could take responsibility for our actions.

Instead of offering unsolicited advice to others, we could offer encouragement and a listening ear.

Instead of indulging in gossip about others, we could keep our focus on the habits we need to change in our own lives.

Instead of making jokes at the expense of others, we could seek to understand our feelings of inferiority.

Instead of telling ourselves we are stupid, lazy, ugly, fat, mean, and not doing enough, we could acknowledge our positive qualities.

The Word of God is reassuring and comforting. The Word of God teaches us that we are all precious children of God, worthy of respect and compassion. The Word of God leads us to explore our hearts in an ongoing adventure of learning to love ourselves and others unconditionally. The Word of God has the power to transform the human condition.

Ponder: How do my words reflect God's Word of love and acceptance?

Prayer: Lord, your Word brings everlasting life. Help me to choose words that spread your loving reassurance, compassion, peace, and healing.

Practice: Today I will tell myself something I like about myself.

Saturday of the First Week in Ordinary Time

YEAR I

Hebrews 4:12–16
Psalm 19:8, 9, 10, 15

YEAR II

1 Samuel 9:1–4, 17–19; 10:1
Psalm 21:2–3, 4–5, 6–7

YEARS I AND II

Mark 2:13–17

As he sat at dinner in Levi's house, many tax collectors and sinners were also sitting with Jesus and his disciples—for there were many who followed him.

MARK 2:15

Reflection: Jesus doesn't like any wall or barrier that blocks the love and compassion of God. He spends intimate moments with people from every background and social condition. He shows us that every person is worthy of God's personal attention.

Sometimes people in our lives are conniving, selfish, and ungrateful. Sometimes people in our lives ignore our needs and take advantage of our good nature. Sometimes people in our lives persecute us, tell lies about us, and destroy our reputation.

God loves everyone equally, even though we don't.

Sometimes people in our lives are pompous and overbearing. Sometimes people in our lives cheat on exams and plagiarize texts. Sometimes people in our lives deliberately embarrass us, hoping to cause us to lose our sense of self-worth.

God loves everyone with their human imperfections, even when we can't.

Sometimes we look down on people because of their culture, race, or socioeconomic background. Sometimes we avoid people because they seem boring, dreary, or self-centered. Sometimes we are annoyed with people who have dementia, learning disabilities, or physical disabilities.

God knows we are frail human beings. God forgives our mistakes and failings. God calls us to learn from the example of Jesus. God invites us to spend intimate moments with the Lord so that we may learn to love ourselves and our sisters and brothers more generously and gracefully.

Ponder: When do I spend intimate time with God?

Prayer: Lord, you love us all. Open my eyes to see my sisters and brothers with eyes of love instead of eyes that judge.

Practice: Today I will eat a meal at a community supper.

Second Sunday in Ordinary Time

YEAR A
Isaiah 49:3, 5–6
Psalm 40:2, 4, 7–8, 8–9, 10
1 Corinthians 1:1–3
John 1:29–34

"I will give you as a light to the nations, that my salvation may reach to the end of the earth."

ISAIAH 49:6B

Reflection: We need light to see the diversity of the human race. We need light to illuminate our pathway of life. We need light to savor the beauty of God's creation.

Each of us has been created to be a guiding light in the world—not just any light, but the guiding presence of the light of Christ. The light of Christ in our hearts helps us see that every person is made in the image of God. The light of Christ in us helps us discern how to use our gifts and talents. The light of Christ in us inspires us to give praise and thanksgiving for all God has created.

We experience periods in life when we feel confused, lost, and restless about many things and need someone to help us sort things out. We experience times when the meaning and purpose of life slips away and we need someone to reassure us with words of encouragement and wisdom. Whenever we find ourselves stuck in a maze of darkness and self-doubt, we need a caring companion, a close friend, a colleague, or a special person to be our guiding light to wholeness.

Christ's mission on Earth was to give witness to the unconditional love of God and to bring about unity among all people. Since we share in the life of Christ, our mission in life is to be the light of Christ, guiding people in the way of love and peace.

Ponder: Where do I need to be the light of Christ?

Prayer: Lord, may your light of love and peace shine brightly in my heart so that others may come to know of your goodness.

Practice: Today I will not dim the light of others.

YEAR B

1 Samuel 3:3b–10, 19
Psalm 40:2, 4, 7–8, 8–9, 10
1 Corinthians 6:13c–15a, 17–20
John 1:35–42

The next day John again was standing with two of his disciples, and as he watched Jesus walk by, he exclaimed, "Look, here is the Lamb of God!" The two disciples heard him say this, and they followed Jesus. When Jesus turned and saw them following, he said to them, "What are you looking for?" They said to him, "Rabbi" (which translated means Teacher), "where are you staying?" He said to them, "Come and see." They came and saw where he was staying, and they remained with him that day.

JOHN 1:35–39

Reflection: John the Baptist turns the attention of his disciples away from himself and points them in the direction of Jesus, the "Lamb of God." John is aware of his disciples' desire to know and enter into a relationship with Jesus.

In the flow of life, we encounter people whose humble witness to the Gospel provokes the presence of Jesus. These self-effacing persons reawaken in our hearts a curiosity to know and follow Jesus.

We can't give authentic witness to Jesus if we have never had an experience with him. We cannot invite others to come and see someone we don't know. To be an authentic Christian in the world demands a deeper knowledge of the life and teachings of Jesus.

We can encounter Jesus and come to know him in the prayerful reading of the gospels, in the sacraments of the Church, and in serving the needs of the poor. Each of our hearts holds a seed of curiosity, an instinct to know Jesus on a personal level. Like John, we need to provoke the presence of Jesus in all sectors of life, sparking a curiosity in the hearts of others to know and follow Jesus.

Ponder: How do I provoke the presence of God?

Prayer: Lord, draw me close to your heart that I may come to know and love you more deeply.

Practice: Today I will find a Bible and begin to read one of the gospels.

YEAR C

Isaiah 62:1–5
Psalm 96:1–2, 2–3, 7–8, 9–10
1 Corinthians 12:4–11
John 2:1–11

Now there are varieties of gifts, but the same Spirit; and there are varieties of services, but the same Lord; and there are varieties of activities, but it is the same God who activates all of them in everyone. To each is given the manifestation of the Spirit for the common good.

1 CORINTHIANS 12:4–7

Reflection: Paul is appealing to the hearts of the people to live in harmony with one another and to work together for the common good. Paul reminds the church at Corinth that they are no longer members of the material world, but members of the spiritual community of God. Paul's challenge was getting the Christian community to think and act in light of their spiritual reality.

Conflict and division are present in the Church today. Many in the Church find it difficult to remain focused on the works of God in the midst of an increasingly secularized world. We need to remember that we are members of the spiritual community of God. In this community we find equality, unity, mutual love, and peace. Our life with God must be reflected in the way we think and act in the world for the common good of all people.

The work of God must be the work of Christians scattered throughout the world. No human gift is less than or greater than another. The Spirit works in and through every gift to bring about love and unity in the world. All the works of the Church must reflect the compassion of Jesus, the humble servant of God. Every activity carried out by the people of God is activated by the Spirit to accomplish the will of God on Earth. All the gifts, services, and activities of the people of God must be used to build a civilization of love, peace, and compassion.

Ponder: What world am I living in at the moment?

Prayer: Lord, send your Spirit and empower me to use my gifts and talents for the common good of all people.

Practice: Today I will be an instrument of peace and reconciliation.

Monday of the Second Week in Ordinary Time

YEAR I
Hebrews 5:1–10
Psalm 110:1, 2, 3, 4

YEAR II
1 Samuel 15:16–23
Psalm 50:8–9, 16bc–17, 21 and 23

YEARS I AND II
Mark 2:18–22

[Jesus said to them] "No one puts new wine into old wineskins; otherwise, the wine will burst the skins, and the wine is lost, and so are the skins; but one puts new wine into fresh wineskins."

MARK 2:22

Reflection: When we repeat the thought and behavior patterns that keep us stressed and unfulfilled, the wineskin of our life is ready to burst.

Jesus challenges us to discard our old habits of anxiety and doubt and face each day with a new attitude of love and hope. We can face the world with confidence in God's love. We can let go of yesterday's troubles and worries and focus on doing our best today. We can approach our responsibilities with a fresh outlook, trusting that God will show us what to do and how to do it. We can refuse to project into the future and instead put our energy into enjoying all that today offers us.

Jesus shows us a new way of living with God as our source of love and strength. We can bring our fears about finances, bills, and employment to God and wait for guidance. We can go to God when we are tired, lonely, or ill and receive comfort and love. We can sit in solitude with God and rest in the silent healing of God's grace.

When life's pressures, tasks, and requirements make us feel like we are about to implode, we can remember to discard our old way of meeting life's demands and take up the new way that Jesus teaches us: Surrendering to God's will of love of God, ourselves, and our neighbors.

Ponder: What old habits do I need to discard?

Prayer: Lord, you are the new wine of life, love, and peace. Bless me with the willingness to pour out love and joy into the lives of my sisters and brothers.

Practice: Today I will try a new approach to a familiar task.

Tuesday of the Second Week in Ordinary Time

YEAR I
Hebrews 6:10–20
Psalm 111:1–2, 4–5, 9 and 10c

YEAR II
1 Samuel 16:1–13
Psalm 89:20, 21–22, 27–28

YEARS I AND II
Mark 2:23–28

"The sabbath was made for humankind and not humankind for the sabbath; so the Son of Man is lord even of the sabbath."

MARK 2:27–28

Reflection: Unlike the other days, the Sabbath was designed by God to be a day of rest, a day of peace. The contemporary mindset is to ignore the Sabbath teaching, promoting instead a consumerist, materialistic lifestyle. The Sabbath is now controlled by the business world and promoted as one of the ideal days to shop and take care of our personal affairs and unfinished business. God is no longer the center and focus of the Sabbath day.

God created the Sabbath to remind us that everything in the world is connected to a divine source and that life has no meaning apart from its divine origin. The Sabbath gives us the opportunity to set aside time to honor our relationship with God and to be with God. Keeping the Sabbath is meant to be a way of life: resting from egotistic behavior, resting from hateful or resentful thoughts, resting from selfishness and greed, resting from violence, resting from harmful speech, and resting from complacency.

The Sabbath was made for us to renew our commitment to love God and neighbor, to defend life, to promote the dignity of all people, to work for peace, and to protect the environment. The Christian worldview is informed and shaped by the teachings of Jesus. The Sabbath, according to Jesus, was made for humankind and not humankind for the Sabbath.

Jesus redirects our minds and hearts away from ourselves and back toward God. Keeping the Sabbath means keeping God as the center of our lives and never forgetting in whose image we are made.

Ponder: What does Sabbath mean to me?

Prayer: Lord, you are the creator of the Sabbath. Forgive my selfishness and renew my desire to spend more time with you.

Practice: I will encourage my family and friends to pray and keep the Sabbath day holy.

Wednesday of the Second Week in Ordinary Time

YEAR I
Hebrews 7:1–3, 15–17
Psalm 110:1, 2, 3, 4

YEAR II
1 Samuel 17:32–33, 37, 40–51
Psalm 144:1b, 2, 9–10

YEARS I AND II
Mark 3:1–6

Then [Jesus] said to them, "Is it lawful to do good or to do harm on the sabbath, to save life or to kill?" But they were silent.

MARK 3:4

Reflection: Jesus teaches us a new law: the law of love. Whether we are faced with making a decision, carrying out an action, or speaking a word, Jesus calls us to choose the law of love.

To practice the law of love, we need to be aware of our thoughts, our feelings, and the people around us. Love demands our awareness. Love demands our attention to what is happening right now. Love demands a commitment to the moment. Without this awareness, we will act mindlessly, allowing habits of a lifetime to make our choices for us.

When we are unaware, we do not even realize we have choices.

Love calls us to participate in life by opening our eyes and ears to notice those who enter our lives at any given moment. Love calls us to recognize opportunities to stretch out a hand in compassion and comfort. Love calls us to be ready to act on behalf of others in their moment of need.

When we are aware, we can no longer be silent when faced with the question of how to help others. We know that love is the only cure for our world. Only love heals. Only love saves. Only love lifts people from despair, builds healthy relationships, brings comfort, resolves conflicts, and opens the way to peace and harmony.

Ponder: How do I practice the law of love?

Prayer: Lord, you heal me when I come to you. Help me to walk in awareness that I may reach out in love and comfort to my brothers and sisters in need.

Practice: Today I will not be silent when faced with an opportunity to offer a word of comfort or encouragement.

Thursday of the Second Week in Ordinary Time

YEAR I
Hebrews 7:25—8:6
Psalm 40:7–8a, 8b–9, 10, 17

YEAR II
1 Samuel 18:6–9; 19:1–7
Psalm 56:2–3, 9–10a, 10b–11, 12–13

YEARS I AND II
Mark 3:7–12

Consequently [Jesus] is able for all time to save those who approach God through him, since he always lives to make intercession for them.

HEBREWS 7:25

Reflection: Life without some form of personal struggle and suffering does not exist. At times, we can experience bouts of mental anguish, emotional heartache, spiritual confusion, physical pain, and interpersonal conflict. For some people, the experience of not feeling well and being restless is a daily challenge.

When our vision becomes blurred and we have difficulty seeing, we are encouraged to seek an optometrist. When the arteries of our heart become clogged, we consult a cardiologist. When signs of cancer appear in our bodies, we need the expert advice of an oncologist. When diabetes and high blood pressure put our life at risk, we are encouraged to talk to a doctor, watch what we eat, and exercise daily.

When conflict visits our family and personal relationships, we want someone to help us heal the hurt and reconcile differences. When addictions overtake and dominate our lives, we are directed to seek treatment and work closely with a sponsor.

In the spiritual realm, our relationship with God is not always as good as we'd like it to be. We cannot neglect our spiritual lives. If we want to improve our relationship with God, we can turn to Jesus and trust that he will help and guide us. When we experience spiritual anguish and feel disconnected from God, we can turn to Jesus in prayer, asking him to intercede for us and make our life with God whole again.

Ponder: What do I need to bring to Jesus?

Prayer: Lord, you are always at my side in times of trouble. Be with me when I am hurting and struggling.

Practice: I will say the Lord's Prayer for people suffering throughout the world.

Friday of the Second Week in Ordinary Time

YEAR I
Hebrews 8:6–13
Psalm 85:8 and 10, 11–12, 13–14

YEAR II
1 Samuel 24:3–21
Psalm 57:2, 3–4, 6 and 11

YEARS I AND II
Mark 3:13–19

[Jesus] went up the mountain and called to him those whom he wanted, and they came to him.

MARK 3:13

Reflection: Going up a mountain is not like taking a stroll in the park. It requires commitment, fitness, and resolve to climb a mountain. And when we reach the top, the view and sense of achievement are always worth the effort.

As we go through life, we face a wide range of mountains. The mountain of growing up. The mountain of relating to others. The mountain of discerning how to put our gifts and talents to good use. The mountain of illness. The mountain of confronting prejudice. The mountain of injustice.

The mountain of failure. The mountain of success. Even when our outer life appears tidy and predictable, our inner life presents us with a continuously mountainous terrain.

Throughout our lives, we experience peaks of accomplishment, plateaus of rest, and valleys of tranquillity. We come to bogs of sorrow, crevices of loneliness, and sheer walls of suffering. We stumble through patches of indifference, get tangled in the brambles of pride, arrogance, and self-doubt.

Nothing is predictable in our mental, emotional, and spiritual mountain ranges. Life is never dull as we explore new ways to reach the top of our inner mountains. We learn humility as we acknowledge that there's always a new mountain to climb.

Jesus calls us to climb the mountains deep within so that we may see the view of our true self: a beloved child of God, made to love and be loved. Jesus goes up the mountain before us to show us the way; when he calls us, we do our best to come to him.

Ponder: What inner mountain am I climbing today?

Prayer: Lord, you go before me to show me the way of truth and life. Teach me to climb the mountains of life steadily and with trust in your loving care.

Practice: Today I will explore an inner mountain that has seemed too steep to climb.

Saturday of the Second Week in Ordinary Time

YEAR I
Hebrews 9:2–3, 11–14
Psalm 47:2–3, 6–7, 8–9

YEAR II
2 Samuel 1:1–4, 11–12, 19, 23–27
Psalm 80:2–3, 5–7

YEARS I AND II
Mark 3:20–21 (NAB)

Jesus came home.

MARK 3:20

Reflection: Wherever Jesus is, he is our home. Wherever we are, Jesus is with us. God is with us. God's Spirit fills our hearts. Wherever we go, the Spirit goes with us. Wherever the Spirit of God is, we are home.

Home is this moment. This moment is filled with God, and God is our home. God does not wait for us to die to make us a home. God is here and now, filling each moment with love and life. God fills us with love and life in each moment. God makes a home in us in each moment. God is our home in each moment. We are at home in God in each moment.

Each breath we take is filled with God's Spirit.

Each breath is our connection with the life force of God. Each breath is a touch of God. Each breath is our home.

God is eternal. Our home is eternal. There is no need to wonder if there is a place for us in God's eternal home. We are at home now. We are in eternity now. We will never be lost and homeless. God is our reassurance, our strength, our love, our home.

When we wonder if we will ever be at peace and feel at home, all we need to do is take a breath and feel God's Spirit in us. All we need to do is open our hearts to God's comfort. All we need to do is rest in the moment, in God's loving embrace, at home with God.

We are at home. Now. In this moment. With God forever.

Ponder: When do I feel at home?

Prayer: Lord, wherever you are is my home. Help me to feel at home with you.

Practice: Today I will spend one minute feeling my breath go in and out and know that I am home.

Third Sunday In Ordinary Time

YEAR A

Isaiah 8:23—9:3
Psalm 27:1, 4, 13–14
1 Corinthians 1:10–13, 17
Matthew 4:12–23 or 4:12–17

Now I appeal to you, brothers and sisters, by the name of our Lord Jesus Christ, that all of you be in agreement and that there be no divisions among you, but that you be united in the same mind and the same purpose.

1 CORINTHIANS 1:10

Reflection: One of the greatest challenges in today's world is finding leaders who can create a community of people united in the same mind and the same purpose. Getting people to put aside their own agendas in favor of the common good requires leaders who possess extraordinary patience, an ability to communicate and collaborate with people from various backgrounds, and an understanding of the art of spiritual discernment and compassionate diplomacy.

It is not unusual for us to be involved in some sort of conflict. Husbands and wives disagree about how to raise their children. Pastors and congregants differ over matters of church governance. College roommates dispute over respecting personal space. Disagreements are a part of life. We need to do our best to resolve whatever keeps people divided against one another.

On a global scale, conflict and division among nations lead to violence and war, which have devastating consequences. When people from different ethnic groups and tribes fail to resolve their conflicts, people are dislocated from their homeland, end up living in poverty and misery, die of hunger and disease, and lose hope.

Saint Paul's pastoral letter to the Corinthians summoned Christians to honor their new life in Christ and to live in accordance with the Spirit of God. God is not divided. God is love. Love is the source of peace and unity. Christian leaders are called to cultivate in the minds and hearts of people God's purpose for humanity: universal love and peace.

Ponder: Am I a source of conflict or peace?

Prayer: Lord, you are the source of peace and unity. Fill me with the desire and courage to be your instrument of peace and love.

Practice: Today I will make amends to someone I have offended.

YEAR B

Jonah 3:1–5, 10
Psalm 25:4–5, 6–7, 8–9
1 Corinthians 7:29–31
Mark 1:14–20

As Jesus passed along the Sea of Galilee, he saw Simon and his brother Andrew casting a net into the sea – for they were fishermen. And Jesus said to them, "Follow me and I will make you fish for people." And immediately they left their nets and followed him.

MARK 1:16–18

Reflection: Simon and his brother were comfortable in their job. They were busy doing what they were trained to do: catch fish. With all their mind, heart, soul, and strength, these fishermen earned a living to provide for their families.

On the surface, leaving a job to follow a stranger does not make sense. Yet Simon and Andrew and all the others called by Jesus learned how to fish for people by listening to the teachings of Jesus and watching his work among the people.

Some people get up each morning to go to a job; they do what they were trained to do. Some people get up each morning to go in search of a job so they can earn a living and take care of their families. Whether employed or unemployed, we are invited to do the work of God. God needs faithful workers to help build the kingdom of God on Earth.

Each day our work is to give witness to the Word of God. Training for this work requires a commitment to prayerfully read the Word of God and be mindful enough to share the wisdom of God's teaching with others.

Catching people is like catching fish. We need to be patient. We catch people for the kingdom of God with the grace-filled Word of God. When we set out to do the work of God, we go with the bait of love, compassion, peace, and forgiveness in our hearts, hoping to attract people to Jesus.

Ponder: What is the meaning and purpose of my work?

Prayer: Lord, you call me to do the work of God in the world. Help me to say yes to your work of peace and reconciliation.

Practice: I will share today's reflection with a friend or colleague.

YEAR C

Nehemiah 8:2–4a, 5–6, 8–10
Psalm 19:8, 9, 10, 15
1 Corinthians 12:12–30 or 12:12–14, 27
Luke 1:1–4; 4:14–21

For in the one Spirit we were all baptized into one body—Jews or Greeks, slaves or free—and we were all made to drink of one Spirit.

1 CORINTHIANS 12:13

Reflection: When parents in the neighborhood do not work together to instill in their children a sense of love and respect for others, hatred of others prevails. When teachers do not work together to create a positive learning environment, children and youth become indifferent to the search for knowledge and truth. When law-enforcement officers do not work together to uphold the law, people in the community begin to administer their own brand of justice. When health-care professionals do not work together to care for the sick and poor, people's lives are put at risk. When members of the business community do not work together to create networks of support, the quality of life diminishes. When Christian religious leaders do not work together to give a common witness to the Gospel of Jesus, people begin to lose faith and hope in God.

All who are baptized receive the Spirit of God's love and belong to the one body of Christ. We have been given the Spirit of God's love to work together to build a community of love. The mission of the Christian community is to use its resources to eradicate the evil of racism in the world, eliminate all forms of violence, and give testimony to the gospel of peace and nonviolence.

Living in the world from the God zone is not easy. Being a member of the body of Christ is not a luxury but a responsibility to be embraced and lived. When Christians work together in accordance with the Spirit of God's love, life becomes more peaceful, fruitful, and loving for all people.

Ponder: How do I live life in the God zone?

Prayer: Lord, you created all people equal. Open my eyes to recognize the dignity of all people and my heart to love unconditionally.

Practice: Today I will reflect on the meaning of my baptism.

Monday of the Third Week in Ordinary Time

YEAR I
Hebrews 9:15, 24–28
Psalm 98:1, 2–3ab, 3cd–4, 5–6

YEAR II
2 Samuel 5:1–7, 10
Psalm 89:20, 21–22, 25–26

YEARS I AND II
Mark 3:22–30

[Jesus spoke to them], "Whoever blasphemes against the Holy Spirit can never have forgiveness, but is guilty of an eternal sin"—for they had said, "He has an unclean spirit."

MARK 3:29–30

Reflection: Deep inside us dwells God's Holy Spirit—pure, innocent, and vibrating with love and joy. Every time we breathe, we are reminded of the Spirit's moving in us. Every time we breathe, we are renewed in the Holy Spirit of healing and compassion. Every time we breathe, we know we are one with the mystery of God's boundless love. The Holy Spirit gives us life, guides our way, and shows us how to become more God-like in our relations with others. Nothing we do can ever sully the perfection of the Holy Spirit.

It takes awareness to recognize our intimate relationship with the Holy Spirit. We can nurture this relationship by treating ourselves and others with kindness and respect. We can foster peace with others by taking the time to listen to the Holy Spirit in our hearts before speaking or acting. We can acknowledge our need for guidance and wisdom by asking the Holy Spirit to discern God's will.

As we grow in awareness of God's Holy Spirit within us, we become more grateful for God's constant presence and compassionate care for us. We become more conscious of God's Spirit moving in others. We become less centered on ourselves and more aware of the needs of others, especially the poor and forgotten. We grow in grace and in the ability to reflect our image of God's love and goodness in the world.

Ponder: How has God's Spirit been a loving guide for me?

Prayer: Lord, your Spirit brings light and love to my life. Help me to show reverence to all people in honor of the indwelling Spirit.

Practice: Today I will ask the Holy Spirit to show me what to do and how to do it.

Tuesday of the Third Week in Ordinary Time

YEAR I
Hebrews 10:1–10
Psalm 40:2 and 4ab, 7–8a, 10, 11

YEAR II
2 Samuel 6:12b–15, 17–19
Psalm 24:7, 8, 9, 10

YEARS I AND II
Mark 3:31–35

[Jesus said] "Whoever does the will of God is my brother and sister and mother."

MARK 3:35

Reflection: God's will is simple: To love God with all our heart, soul, and mind, and to love our neighbor as ourselves. Doing the will of God unites us as God's family.

A community made up of people with a common mindset, a common purpose, and a common goal creates a powerful presence. When our mindset, purpose, and goal are to love God, ourselves, and our neighbors without exception, our community is brother, sister, and mother to Jesus.

In this kind of community, everyone is a teacher and everyone is a student. Our elder people bring wisdom and the experience of forgiveness to the community. Our young people bring energy, vision, and vitality to the community. Our middle-aged people bring a sense of continuity and a bridge of caring between the generations. No one person ever has all the answers or experience we need. We need all of our people.

A community based on the law of God's love is grounded in humility. We know we are dependent on God. We know that God gives us the intellect, courage, creativity, and longing to be a loving presence in the world. We know that when we forget to keep God in the center of our lives and our community, we have forgotten our common purpose.

A community of people devoted to bringing love to a troubled, spiritually starving world can only become a reality when we intentionally choose to be in relationship with God. When we consciously seek to know God's will for us in every moment and ask God for the grace to carry it out, we are on our way to being brother, sister, and mother to Jesus.

Ponder: Where am I doing God's will in my life?

Prayer: Here I am, Lord. I come to do your will.

Practice: Today I will seek time with God and ask to be shown God's will for me.

Wednesday of the Third Week in Ordinary Time

YEAR I
Hebrews 10:11–18
Psalm 110:1, 2, 3, 4

YEAR II
2 Samuel 7:4–17
Psalm 89:4–5, 27–28, 29–30

YEARS I AND II
Mark 4:1–20

Again [Jesus] began to teach beside the sea. Such a very large crowd gathered around him that he got into a boat on the sea and sat there, while the whole crowd was beside the sea on the land. He began to teach them many things in parables, and in his teaching he said to them: "Listen! A sower went out to sow."

MARK 4:1–3

Reflection: Words have power; they affect people's lives. The words Jesus spoke moved people. Many gathered to hear what Jesus had to say because he was able to touch their hearts and relate to their human condition.

When Jesus spoke about the goodness, love, compassion, forgiveness, and peace of God, he opened the eyes and ears of the people's hearts to a different vision of life, one that would bear much fruit.

Those who listened to and reflected on the words of Jesus came to know that Jesus is the Son of God who came to lead us to the kingdom of God. Jesus always challenged people to look at life from God's perspective.

Our words have power; they affect people's lives. Empowered by the Word of God, we are called to sow words that promote the common good, nonviolence, love, compassion, the sacredness of life, and the dignity of all people.

Sometimes we underestimate the power of our words. We are unaware of how our words affect people's lives and that what we say has consequences. We use words to convey meaning, express our feelings and thoughts, give direction, call attention to important matters, warn of impending danger, encourage and support. More people will be open to listening to us and believing in the Word of God when our actions match what we sow with our words.

Ponder: Do I think before I speak?

Prayer: Lord, you are the source of my life. May your words bring comfort and peace to my life.

Practice: Today I will listen more and speak less.

Thursday of the Third Week in Ordinary Time

YEAR I
Hebrews 10:19–25
Psalm 24:1–2, 3–4ab, 5–6

YEAR II
2 Samuel 7:18–19, 24–29
Psalm 132:1–2, 3–5, 11, 12, 13–14

YEARS I AND II
Mark 4:21–25

[Jesus] said to them, "Is a lamp brought in to be put under the bushel basket, or under the bed, and not on the lampstand? For there is nothing hidden, except to be disclosed; nor is anything secret, except to come to light."

MARK 4:21–22

Reflection: We all shine with the light of God's love. We all have the brilliance of God's Holy Spirit within us, giving us the power to act as beacons of peace, hope, and love to all those we encounter.

Sometimes our light seems feeble. Life has challenged us to where we feel worn down. We've experienced rejection, loss, injustice, unfaithfulness, deceit, and persecution. We've been through pain, illness, unemployment, divorce, incarceration, and bankruptcy. We've been depressed and unhappy— and felt our life was useless.

Yet when we examine our lives with the perspective of awareness, we notice that everything that happens is just an experience. And every experience is an opportunity to be aware of our human frailty, to accept our need for God's love and guidance, to ask God to walk with us through the experience instead of dodging it.

Our inner light is always fed by the Holy Spirit, by an endless source of love and truth. Our challenge is to embrace our human experiences rather than feel victimized by them. Our challenge is to relish our humanity rather than reject it. Our challenge is to let our light of love, hope, and faith shine, especially when life's unfortunate circumstances seem too dark to penetrate.

Ponder: How, when, and where do I let my light shine in the world?

Prayer: Lord, you have filled us with the light of your Holy Spirit. Teach me to let go of fear and doubt and to shine the light of love and hope wherever I go.

Practice: Today I will use one of my gifts and talents to help someone in need.

Friday of the Third Week in Ordinary Time

YEAR I
Hebrews 10:32–39
Psalm 37:3–4, 5–6, 23–24, 39–40

YEAR II
2 Samuel 11:1–4a, 5–10a, 13–17
Psalm 51:3–4, 5–6a, 6bcd–7, 10–11

YEARS I AND II
Mark 4:26–34

With many such parables [Jesus] spoke the word to them, as they were able to hear it.

MARK 4:33

Reflection: Jesus talks to the people in words they understand. He talks about seeds, harvests, mustard shrubs, and birds because the people have experience of them. Jesus wants the people to understand about God's love, and so he tells them stories that will bring God's love alive for them and make it real to them.

God's love is real. God's love is available to us in every moment. God loves each of us personally, tenderly, and intensely. God forgives us for our human errors. God is with us to heal our doubts and to give us the courage to keep on doing our best to be like God.

God's love is tangible. We can experience God's love in the beauty and bounty of creation. We can experience God's love in the gentle touch of a person. We can experience God's love in sacred Scripture. We can experience God's love in the celebration of the Eucharist.

God's love is an incomprehensible mystery. Who can understand a boundless, unconditional love that enters the mind, heart, and soul of each and every human person? But Jesus never intends the reality of God's love to elude us. Jesus wants us to understand that God loves us unconditionally and that we have the seed of God's love in us. Jesus uses the story of a tiny seed that has the potential to grow into an enormous shrub to teach us that we have the power to make the seed of God's love in us grow and become a haven for others.

Ponder: How do I nurture the seed of God's love in me?

Prayer: Lord, your love is real. Help me to tell the story of your love with every word I speak and every action I take.

Practice: Today I will speak words of love and encouragement wherever I go.

Saturday of the Third Week in Ordinary Time

YEAR I
Hebrews 11:1–2, 8–19
Luke 1:69–70, 71–72, 73–75

YEAR II
2 Samuel 12:1–7a, 10–17
Psalm 51:12–13, 14–15, 16–17

YEARS I AND II
Mark 4:35–41

A great windstorm arose, and the waves beat into the boat, so that the boat was already being swamped. But [Jesus] was in the stern, asleep on the cushion.

MARK 4:37–38

Reflection: Being human is tiring. Feeling our emotions, keeping up with our runaway thoughts, performing the many chores and tasks required of us, and relating to others are ways we pour out our energy. In addition, our nervous system is constantly processing energy from a number of other sources, such as cell phones, televisions, computers, iPods, microwaves, weed whackers, traffic, chemically treated water and food, and barometric pressure.

Jesus shows us that we all need time to rest in the

windstorms of life. There is nothing shameful in taking a break. There is no harm in turning off the phone. There is no need to be available twenty-four hours a day. Our bodies, minds, and spirits demand alone time to rest and be renewed and refreshed.

Sometimes we think we have to keep going and keep doing more. We think our constant busyness or availability will prove our worth or make us successful. Although that type of outlook may fit a modern business model, it is not the model Jesus shows us. Jesus shows us it's all right to take a break even when storms are raging.

Sometimes we cling to our busyness because we think being in constant connection with others will chase away the deep loneliness inside. Jesus shows us that reconnecting with ourselves is the cure for loneliness and will make us whole again.

Jesus teaches us the simple truth that taking downtime is an expression of self-love. And from that space of self-love and renewal, we find the compassion and energy to continue pouring out in service to God and others.

Ponder: When do I take downtime?

Prayer: Lord, you are human and divine. Teach me to follow your example that I may grow more like you.

Practice: Today I will rest when I am tired.

Fourth Sunday in Ordinary Time

YEAR A

Zephaniah 2:3; 3:12–13
Psalm 146:6–7, 8–9, 9–10
1 Corinthians 1:26–31
Matthew 5:1–12a

"Blessed are the pure in heart, for they will see God."

MATTHEW 5:8

Reflection: The home is no longer the centerpiece and heart of our society. It has been replaced by shopping malls, coffee shops, fitness centers, and other social venues. In our fast-paced society, we are restless and find it difficult to stay at home. We are always on the go, moving from one activity to the next. Even when we are at home, we struggle to find time to reflect on life, to be with others, to talk about life experiences, to share intimate thoughts and feelings, and to pray together.

On a deeper level, we are restless creatures who do not feel at home in our own hearts. We fear and resist the call to self-discovery. Becoming self-aware may provoke too much confusion, too much inner work, too much pain, and too much personal responsibility. Rather than be confronted by the inner truth that resides in our heart, we run away from it in search of false happiness and security.

When we are "pure in heart" we are not afraid to take up residence in our own hearts, acknowledging that our true home is with God. We are at peace with God.

We need to pay more attention to our relationship with God, who dwells in our hearts. In our hyperactive, hyperconnected lifestyle, we tend to become disconnected from God and from what God means in our lives: love, peace, compassion, and forgiveness. If we want to see God and understand ourselves better, then we need to come in from the world and spend more time at home with God in our hearts.

Ponder: Why am I so restless in my life?

Prayer: Lord, you dwell in the depth of my being. May your Spirit help me to seek and to know you with all my heart, mind, soul, and strength.

Practice: Today I will find a quiet place to reflect on my relationship with God.

YEAR B

Deuteronomy 18:15–20
Psalm 95:1–2, 6–7, 7–9
1 Corinthians 7:32–35
Mark 1:21–28

"What is this? A new teaching—with authority! He commands even the unclean spirits, and they obey him." At once [Jesus'] fame began to spread throughout the surrounding region of Galilee.

MARK 1:27B–28

Reflection: Since Jesus is God, he possesses divine power. When Jesus speaks, he speaks with the authority of God. God's word has the power to drive out every unclean spirit, thus making all things new.

The Christian community that prayerfully reads and acts on the Word of God has the power to drive out any unclean spirits that rob the Earth and humanity of their intrinsic goodness and dignity.

The Gospel gives us some insight into what it means to be a Christian witness in the world today. We can live and work in the world with the strength and power of the Word of God in our hearts, knowing that God's Word of peace, love, compassion, and forgiveness can overcome all the hatred and bitterness that keep people apart.

When we are filled with the healing power of

God's Word, we can offer compassion to the poor by using our gifts, talents, and resources to feed the hungry throughout the world. We have the power to restore lives and eradicate global poverty.

When we are illuminated with the wisdom of God's Word, we can give witness to our faith in God by being actively engaged in those activities that promote life and the nonviolent development of all peoples.

When we are guided by the transformative Spirit of God's Word, we can be lights of hope and liberate people from the unclean spirits of despair, fear, loneliness, and rejection.

When we faithfully live the Word of God each day, we help to spread the kingdom of God everywhere.

Ponder: What does it mean for me to be a Christian in today's world?

Prayer: Lord, you created me to live in the freedom of your love. Give me the courage to share your love with all people.

Practice: Today I will carry a positive attitude in my heart.

YEAR C

Jeremiah 1:4–5, 17–19
Psalm 71:1–2, 3–4, 5–6, 15, 17
1 Corinthians 12:31—13:13 or 13:4–13
Luke 4:21–30

Love is patient; love is kind; love is not envious or boastful or arrogant or rude. It does not insist on its own way; it is not irritable or resentful; it does not rejoice in wrongdoing, but rejoices in the truth. It bears all things, believes all things, hopes all things, endures all things.

1 CORINTHIANS 13:4–7

Reflection: Each of us is aware that life is not tidy. Family members don't always get along, next-door neighbors quarrel with one another, pastors and parishioners often disagree over doctrinal and pastoral issues, teachers and students sometimes don't share the same values, people from different racial and ethnic groups hate one another, creating conflict and tension.

Saint Paul's teaching on love helps each of us strive for the "more excellent way" and to do our best to be a more perfect lover in an imperfect world.

Saint Paul reminds us that the foundation of life is love; that the essence of the Christian life is love. No matter what happens in life, love is supreme.

When we are in conflict with others, we must seek to love. When we are hurt by someone, especially a family member, we must find a way to love and offer forgiveness. When we are becoming selfish and materialistic, we need to reclaim love and be more generous to the poor and needy.

When we are prejudiced toward others because of their race, ethnic background, religious beliefs, political stance, gender, or way of life, we need to remember to love and be more open, respectful, and understanding.

Saint Paul's vision of love is not a lofty, unreachable goal. It is the real work Christians are called to do in the world. Our faith is grounded in a divine love that never fails, no matter what circumstances we face in this life.

Ponder: Do I love all people unconditionally?

Prayer: Lord, your love never fails. Help me to embrace life with gratitude and love and joyfully welcome all people into my heart.

Practice: Today I will be less judgmental of others.

Monday of the Fourth Week in Ordinary Time

YEAR I
Hebrews 11:32–40
Psalm 31:20, 21, 22, 23, 24

YEAR II
2 Samuel 15:13–14, 30; 16:5–13
Psalm 3:2–3, 4–5, 6–7

YEARS I AND II
Mark 5:1–20

As [Jesus] was getting into the boat, the man who had been possessed by demons begged him that he might be with him. But Jesus refused, and said to him, "Go home to your friends, and tell them how much the Lord has done for you, and what mercy he has shown you."

MARK 5:18–19

Reflection: God is paying attention to us at every moment. We are receiving God's gifts of mercy, forgiveness, peace, and love with every breath. Our awareness is not usually on the moment, however, and we tend to let God's gifts pass by unnoticed. Our awareness is usually on the worry of the day, the gossip of the hour, the past, or the future. We rarely dwell in the present. We seldom step into the spaciousness of *now* to enjoy the gift of God's presence.

When Jesus refuses to let the man who had been possessed by Legion come with him, he directs him to a different path: To live his everyday life aware of God's presence, God's gifts, and God's mercy—and to share that awareness with his friends.

Sharing our awareness of God's gifts with others involves opening our hearts to gratitude: gratitude for family and friends, gratitude for a job, gratitude for eyes that see and ears that hear, gratitude for the beauty of nature, gratitude for our gifts and talents. Gratitude even for hardship and grief that make us turn to God for comfort and healing.

Jesus honors our everyday experience by asking us to become aware of God's presence in everything that happens to us. Jesus asks us to build the kingdom of God by sharing our knowledge and joy in God's presence.

Ponder: What has the Lord done for me?

Prayer: Lord, my hope is in you. Make me aware of and grateful for your loving presence in each moment.

Practice: Today I will make a gratitude list.

Tuesday of the Fourth Week in Ordinary Time

YEAR I

Hebrews 12:1–4
Psalm 22:26b–27, 28 and 30, 31–32

YEAR II

2 Samuel 18:9–10, 14b, 24–25a, 30—19:3
Psalm 86:1–2, 3–4, 5–6

YEARS I AND II

Mark 5:21–43

Then one of the leaders of the synagogue named Jairus came and, when he saw [Jesus], fell at his feet and begged him repeatedly, "My little daughter is at the point of death. Come and lay your hands on her, so that she may be made well, and live."

MARK 5:22–23

Reflection: Jesus shows great love and compassion to all who are suffering and in pain, especially little children. He teaches us that children are to be given every chance to live a full, meaningful, and productive life.

There are children throughout the world who are dying due to the lack of food, water, medicine, and shelter. There are children whose minds hunger to learn to read and write, but there are no schools for them to attend. There are children abandoned by their parents who are looking for a family to take them in. There are children dislocated from their homeland because of violence and war. There are children who have been forced to become prostitutes, soldiers, and slaves who long for a new life.

We cannot ignore the plight of these children throughout the world. It is our Christian duty to be the presence of God's love and compassion to the poor, the suffering, and to all who are near death. Inspired by the life and ministry of Jesus, we need to help alleviate the suffering of all children.

Every child is a gift from God. Jesus came into the world with the resources of love and compassion to heal the sick and comfort those who are suffering and in pain. We, too, have what we need to make sure any child can be given a chance to live a healthy and prosperous life.

Ponder: What have I done to help children at risk?

Prayer: Lord, you embrace and bless little children. Heal and make whole my inner child.

Practice: Today I will become familiar with a project or organization that addresses the needs of children.

Wednesday of the Fourth Week in Ordinary Time

YEAR I
Hebrews 12:4–7, 11–15
Psalm 103:1–2, 13–14, 17–18a

YEAR II
2 Samuel 24:2, 9–17
Psalm 32:1–2, 5, 6, 7

YEARS I AND II
Mark 6:1–6

Then Jesus said to them, "Prophets are not without honor, except in their hometown, and among their own kin, and in their own house." And he could do no deed of power there, except that he laid his hands on a few sick people and cured them.

MARK 6:4–5

Reflection: One of our greatest adventures in life is getting to know other people. Each of us is a mystery to be explored. We have hidden facets that we ourselves may not yet have come across. In a world where it appears there are no new frontiers, we come to realize that every person we meet is an unknown territory worthy of discovery and study.

Usually, however, our tendency is to learn just enough about others so that we feel safe with them. From what we learn, we tend to label someone as easygoing, irritable, arrogant, kind, stupid, crazy, or fun.

Our need to label others is a reflection of our insecurity. When someone steps out of the box and acts differently from what we expect, we feel threatened. We might feel the need to criticize, belittle, or condemn the other person. Yet our need to label means we are missing an opportunity to explore and experience the true mystery of the person.

Jesus shows us that we try to label even God. We think we know who God is. We are frightened by the vastness of God's love, wisdom, and power, and so we restrict God's movement in our lives by clinging to our preconceived definition of God. When we learn to welcome the mystery of God into our minds and hearts, letting go of all our limiting beliefs, new frontiers and new adventures will open up for us.

Ponder: How do I try to control God?

Prayer: Lord, I am in awe of you. Help me to explore the mystery of your love with joy and confidence.

Practice: Today I will talk to someone I usually avoid.

Thursday of the Fourth Week in Ordinary Time

YEAR I
Hebrews 12:18–19, 21–24
Psalm 48:2–3ab, 3cd–4, 9, 10–11

YEAR II
1 Kings 2:1–4, 10–12
1 Chronicles 29:10, 11ab, 11d–12a, 12bcd

YEARS I AND II
Mark 6:7–13

[Jesus] ordered them to take nothing for their journey except a staff; no bread, no bag, no money in their belts; but to wear sandals and not to put on two tunics.

MARK 6:8–9

Reflection: Jesus is teaching his disciples a different style of leadership, one that embraces love of God and neighbor along with a humble lifestyle.

As followers of Jesus, we must not be distracted by worldly things. We have been called to carry the Word of God in our hearts; our mission is to preach and teach the Word of God. Christian discipleship challenges us to simplify our lives so that we will not be weighed down by our material possessions.

It's hard to think about the Word of God when we are overwhelmed by the anxieties of life.

Christian discipleship requires that we strengthen our relationship with God by reading and reflecting on the Word of God. We cannot give to others what we do not possess in our hearts. We must be ready to bring to the human condition the unambiguous message of love, compassion, peace, and forgiveness proclaimed by Jesus. Grounded in the Word of God, we can provoke God's presence in the public arena, giving believers and unbelievers an opportunity to reflect on the meaning of human existence.

In a world in which the message of God's love is being overtaken by messages of greed, hatred of others, and violence, we must not be afraid to share the Word of God with others in a spirit of humility and peace. Christian discipleship is the work of transforming the minds and hearts of people with the Word of God.

Ponder: How do I share the Word of God with others?

Prayer: Lord, your Word brings about new life. May your Spirit inspire me to share a message of hope and love with all people.

Practice: Today I will offer love and support to someone in need.

Friday of the Fourth Week in Ordinary Time

YEAR I
Hebrews 13:1–8
Psalm 27:1, 3, 5, 8b–9abc

YEAR II
Sirach 47:2–11
Psalm 18:31, 47 and 50, 51

YEARS I AND II
Mark 6:14–29

King Herod heard of it, for Jesus' name had become known. Some were saying, "John the baptizer has been raised from the dead; and for this reason these powers are at work in him."

MARK 6:14

Reflection: People are talking about Jesus. They are speculating about who he is, what he's doing, and the source of his healing powers. Gossip about Jesus is intense and widespread. People are lining up to touch his cloak and beg for healing. Jesus is the star of the moment, the answer to people's prayers, a compassionate, healing presence in a troubled, turbulent society.

What has happened to that intense interest in the

work of Jesus? Where has the excitement about Jesus gone? Why have we stopped talking to one another about the good Jesus does for us? Are we anxious to seek Jesus out? Do we long to touch him and ask for healing? Do we believe Jesus is here for us still? Can we feel the power of Jesus even though our world is troubled and turbulent? What will it take to make Jesus the star of the moment, of every moment?

We tend to live without awareness of the power of God in and around us. Our conscious contact with God is superficial, lukewarm, and intermittent. We are sluggish and lack initiative when it comes to getting to know Jesus better. If we want to regain the excitement that made people talk and speculate about Jesus during his physical lifetime, we need to spend time deliberately getting to know Jesus. We need to spend intimate time with Jesus. We need to become aware of Jesus within us.

Ponder: When have I been excited about Jesus?

Prayer: Your presence, O Lord, I seek. Help me to know you better that I may speak from my heart about your goodness and love.

Practice: Today I will spend five minutes listening to Jesus.

Saturday of the Fourth Week in Ordinary Time

YEAR I
Hebrews 13:15–17, 20–21
Psalm 23:1–3a, 3b–4, 5, 6

YEAR II
1 Kings 3:4–13
Psalm 119:9, 10, 11, 12, 13, 14

YEARS I AND II
Mark 6:30–34

As [Jesus] went ashore, he saw a great crowd; and he had compassion for them, because they were like sheep without a shepherd; and he began to teach them many things.

MARK 6:34

Reflection: Faced with a great crowd of people just when he is ready to rest, Jesus sees beyond the surface and understands that the people want to learn from him. He knows we are all searching for understanding, peace, and love. He knows that, left to ourselves, we will wander like sheep, making a mess everywhere we go. Jesus willingly teaches us so that we will become more like him, especially in our relations with others.

Jesus loves all people. He teaches us to love ourselves and our neighbors.

Jesus has compassion for all people. He teaches us to have compassion for ourselves and our neighbors.

Jesus shepherds all people on the path of peace, reconciliation, and love. He teaches us to walk the same path and to invite our neighbors to walk with us.

Jesus listens to the cries of the poor and forgotten. He teaches us to listen to the poor and forgotten with our hearts as well as our ears, and to reach out to help those in need.

Jesus dines with sinners. He teaches us to break bread with people from all religions, nations, races, and walks of life.

Jesus speaks out against injustice. He teaches us to speak out in defense of those who cannot or do not know how to speak for themselves.

Jesus teaches at every moment, in every situation. He teaches us to let our words, our actions, and our lives teach others that God is here with us, ever present, ever patient, ever loving.

Ponder: What does Jesus teach me?

Prayer: Lord, teach me your decrees. Help me follow your example that I may not stray from your path of love and reconciliation.

Practice: Today I will let compassion be my response to all people.

Fifth Sunday in Ordinary Time

YEAR A

Isaiah 58:7–10
Psalm 112:4–5, 6–7, 8–9
1 Corinthians 2:1–5
Matthew 5:13–16

"You are the salt of the earth; but if salt
has lost its taste, how can its saltiness be
restored? It is no longer good for anything,
but is thrown out and trampled under foot."

MATTHEW 5:13

Reflection: It is God's will that we use our gifts
and talents for some good purpose. To be salt of
the earth is to be God's instrument of peace, love,
and compassion.

We are salt of the earth when we take time to
acknowledge and greet others rather than pass them
by because we are in a rush and cannot be bothered.
We are salt of the earth when we take time to thank
someone who has been kind to us rather than walk
away with an ungrateful heart. We are salt of the
earth when we find time to listen to a person's painful story rather than be indifferent.

We are salt of the earth when we share our bread
with the hungry rather than waste food. We are salt
of the earth when we clothe the naked rather than

buy more things for ourselves. We are salt of the earth when we do not turn our back on the homeless but rather do our part to help them find shelter.

We are salt of the earth when we stop speaking ill of others and do our best to find goodness in people regardless of their race, ethnic background, or sexual orientation. We are salt of the earth when we refrain from hurting others and make amends with those who have hurt us.

We are salt of the earth when our actions are motivated by love of God and neighbor. The Christian life will never lose its taste as long as it is rooted in the Word of God.

Ponder: How do I use my gifts and talents?

Prayer: Lord, you have blessed the world with goodness and love. Help me to use my gifts and talents in accordance with your will.

Practice: Today I will take a personal inventory of my gifts and talents.

YEAR B

Job 7:1–4, 6–7
Psalm 147:1–2, 3–4, 5–6
1 Corinthians 9:16–19, 22–23
Mark 1:29–39

In the morning, while it was still very dark, [Jesus] got up and went out to a deserted place, and there he prayed.

MARK 1:35

Reflection: Jesus was never too busy to make time for prayer. He rose early in the morning and went off to be alone with God.

Prayer was an essential ritual in the life of Jesus. His ministry among the people was grounded in prayer. He prepared to do God's work in solitude, conforming his mind and heart to the will of God. Jesus knew he could not preach about prayer if he was not a prayerful person.

It's difficult to live a Christian spiritual life without prayer. We have nothing to offer if we are not living in prayerful communion with God.

Perhaps one of today's greatest challenges is creating solitude and making time for prayer. Yet a life without prayer is a life out of balance. If we want to appreciate the beauty of creation, we need to pray. If we want to bring order to our disordered lives, we need to pray. If we want to have clarity of thought, we need to pray. If we want to discern what is important in life, we need to pray. If we want to improve our relationship with God and neighbor, we need to pray. If we want a more peaceful, nonviolent world, we need to pray. If we want to live a happy, healthy life, we need to pray. If we want to understand the Word of God, we need to pray. If we want to hear the voice of God within our hearts, we need to pray.

In prayer, our hearts are set free to be with God, who gives us peace and joy.

Ponder: When do I make time for prayer?

Prayer: Lord, you hear the cry of the poor. Hear my cry for inner peace and happiness.

Practice: Today I will find a quiet place and spend time alone with God.

YEAR C
Isaiah 6:1–2a, 3–8
Psalm 138:1–2, 2–3, 4–5, 7–8
1 Corinthians 15:1–11 or 15:3–8, 11
Luke 5:1–11

While Jesus was standing beside the lake of Gennesaret, the crowd was pressing in on him to hear the word of God.

Reflection: Jesus came into the world to reveal the plan of God. Through his preaching and teaching, Jesus offered the people opportunities to reflect on the Word of God. In speaking the Word of God, Jesus made people curious about God. The people who pressed upon Jesus were longing for a message of love, compassion, freedom, and hope in the midst of difficult times. The words Jesus spoke lifted up their human dignity.

We have been called by God, empowered by the Holy Spirit, to carry on the mission of Jesus in the world. Wherever we stand, we have a duty to speak the Word of God with courage. In sharing the Word of God, we make others curious about God, inviting them to reflect on their relationship with God and neighbor.

When people press upon us, we need to be careful not to betray the Word of God that we have listened

Fifth Week in Ordinary Time 87

to in our hearts. Every encounter with a person is an opportunity to convey a message of love, compassion, hope, and peace. As a follower of Jesus, we can use the inspiration of the Word of God to advocate for peace and justice, to call attention to the plight of the poor, to defend the sacredness of all life, to dismantle barriers between people, and to promote the dignity and equality of every person.

The Word of God is not something we leave behind at church or in the privacy of our homes. The Word of God must be carried with us, constantly reflected on in our hearts, so that wherever people press upon us, we are ready to share a message from God.

Ponder: When do I read and reflect on the Word of God?

Prayer: Lord, you are the Word made flesh. Open my heart to share your message of love and hope with the people around me.

Practice: Today I will choose my words carefully when conversing with others.

Monday of the Fifth Week in Ordinary Time

YEAR I
Genesis 1:1–19
Psalm 104:1–2a, 5–6, 10 and 12, 24 and 35c

YEAR II
1 Kings 8:1–7, 9–13
Psalm 132:6–7, 8–10

YEARS I AND II
Mark 6:53–56

And wherever [Jesus] went, into villages or cities or farms, they laid the sick in the marketplaces, and begged him that they might touch even the fringe of his cloak; and all who touched it were healed.

MARK 6:56

Reflection: If people were to touch the fringe of our garment, what would they feel? Would they feel the warmth of love and healing? the sharpness of anger? the cloudiness of despair? the comfort of gratitude? the coldness of complacency? the peace of self-acceptance? the joy of knowing we are beloved of God?

Every day we have the option to put on garments of welcome, encouragement, enjoyment, kindness, and courtesy. We have the opportunity to dress ourselves in peace, understanding, forgiveness, respect, and reconciliation. We have the choice to wear cloaks of helpfulness, generosity, gentleness, patience, and humility.

Wherever we go, we make an impression on others. By our presence alone, we allow others to touch who we really are and to know God through us.

Sometimes we struggle and are afraid to let others know who we really are and to know God within us. Maybe we have been deeply wounded by others' rejection or abuse and do not want to risk being vulnerable. Maybe life's troubles have discouraged us and we use sarcasm, ridicule, or anger to prevent people from seeing our true nature.

Yet whatever our experience in life has been, in every moment we have the power to reach out to touch the cloak of Jesus and experience healing and love. With this gentle gift from God comes the willingness to let our true selves of love and goodness touch the lives of others.

Ponder: When have I allowed others to touch the real me?

Prayer: O Lord, you are clothed in light and love. May I dare to touch you in others and know that we are all your beloved children.

Practice: Today I will put on garments of kindness and respect.

Tuesday of the Fifth Week in Ordinary Time

YEAR I
Genesis 1:20—2:4a
Psalm 8:4–5, 6–7, 8–9

YEAR II
1 Kings 8:22–23, 27–30
Psalm 84:3, 4, 5 and 10, 11

YEARS I AND II
Mark 7:1–13

[Jesus said to the Pharisees and scribes] "You abandon the commandment of God and hold to human tradition."

MARK 7:8

Reflection: The commandment of God is love. Jesus is telling us that love counts more than tradition. Jesus is telling us that if we do not love God and one another, our traditions are empty and meaningless.

About 25 percent of United States Catholics attend Mass on Sunday. The human tradition of requiring attendance at Sunday Mass has great meaning for these members of the faith. And for many Catholics who do not attend Mass regularly, their tradition is to attend Mass on Christmas and Easter. How do we welcome those Catholics who attend Mass only on Christmas or Easter? Do we cheerfully push over in our pew to make room? Do we smile and speak, wishing everyone the joy of the season? Do we offer our seats to parents with young children? How do we practice the law of love at our eucharistic celebrations?

Jesus reminds us to place love above all else. If our traditions exclude others, we need to change them to provide a welcome for all. If our traditions ignore the needs of the poor, we need to change them to provide food for the hungry and shelter for the homeless. If our traditions silence the voice of the people, we need to change them to provide opportunities for all to have a say in the life of the Church. If our traditions diminish the importance of the Word of God and the Eucharist, we need to change them and reset our priorities.

Ponder: What human traditions prevent me from practicing the law of love?

Prayer: Lord, you have blessed us with your unconditional love. Show me how to love my neighbor as myself.

Practice: Today I will create a new tradition of showing love to at least one person a day.

Wednesday of the Fifth Week in Ordinary Time

YEAR I
Genesis 2:4b–9, 15–17
Psalm 104:1–2a, 27–28, 29bc–30

YEAR II
1 Kings 10:1–10
Psalm 37:5–6, 30–31, 39–40

YEARS I AND II
Mark 7:14–23

[And Jesus said] "For it is from within, from the human heart, that evil intentions come: fornication, theft, murder, adultery, avarice, wickedness, deceit, licentiousness, envy, slander, pride, folly."

MARK 7:21–22

Reflection: Jesus teaches us that we are responsible for ourselves. We have the power to choose how we live in this world. We have the power to choose how we relate to others. We have the power to choose our attitudes every day, in every moment. We have the power to make a positive impact in the world.

When we realize the force of our own power and align it with God's will that we love ourselves and our neighbor, our hearts pour forth peace, joy, contentment, forgiveness, compassion, kindness, and respect in the world. We become more able to help the poor, heal the brokenhearted, and visit the sick. We become more willing to listen patiently to others, to offer comfort to the grieving, and to accept the foibles of humanity with tolerance and good humor. We become aware of others' rights and boundaries and refuse to take advantage of the weak. We become grateful for our gifts and talents and learn to appreciate the gifts of others. We become mindful of our dependence on God and let go of arrogance and pride. We become able to bring our needs to God in prayer, to discern God's will for us, and to carry out God's will with energy, courage, and grace.

Taking responsibility for ourselves and making a firm decision to ground ourselves in the love of God bring endless opportunities to proclaim peace, joy, and hope with our very lives.

Ponder: What comes out of my heart?

Prayer: O Lord, your law of love is written in my heart. Teach me to be responsible for myself. Show me how to use the power of your love to help those in need.

Practice: Today I will actively choose to speak peaceful words to all whom I encounter.

Thursday of the Fifth Week in Ordinary Time

YEAR I
Genesis 2:18–25
Psalm 128:1–2, 3, 4–5

YEAR II
1 Kings 11:4–13
Psalm 106:3–4, 35–36, 37 and 40

YEARS I AND II
Mark 7:24–30

But she answered [Jesus], "Sir, even the dogs under the table eat the children's crumbs." Then he said to her, "For saying that, you may go—the demon has left your daughter." So she went home, found the child lying on the bed, and the demon gone.

MARK 7:28–30

Reflection: Our dependence on God is not a patriarchal relationship. God is not "up there," and we are not "down here." We are entwined with God. We live and breathe with God. We rely on God for life, love, and guidance—and God relies on us to show the world who God is. Because we can be visible, tangible proof of God's love and healing, sometimes in the stories of our lives we are the protagonists and

Jesus plays a supporting role—as in this story of the Syrophoenician woman.

Jesus tries to avoid this humble woman, but she draws closer. She shows him a vision of faith and healing that goes beyond his stated ministry to the Jewish people. Jesus picks up the cue and reshapes his ministry to include all people. Together, Jesus and the Syrophoenician woman have made reconciliation and unity an integral part of our mission as followers of Jesus.

Jesus and the Syrophoenician woman show us the power of our relationship with God. When we spend time with Jesus, question him, listen to him, answer him, ask him for guidance, insist that he act on behalf of those in need, and persist in getting to know him, we strengthen our knowledge and wisdom, our love and compassion, our capacity for peace and forgiveness. We open the way for positive change in our world.

Ponder: What am I doing at the moment to bring about positive change in the world?

Prayer: Lord, you are feeding me cues in every moment. Help me to play my role as your partner in manifesting love and peace in our world.

Practice: Today I will be more gentle with people who disrupt my routines.

Friday of the Fifth Week in Ordinary Time

YEAR I
Genesis 3:1–8
Psalm 32:1–2, 5, 6, 7

YEAR II
1 Kings 11:29–32; 12:19
Psalm 81:10–11ab, 12–13, 14–15

YEARS I AND II
Mark 7:31–37

They brought to [Jesus] a deaf man who had an impediment in his speech; and they begged him to lay his hand on him. He took him aside in private, away from the crowd, and put his fingers into his ears, and he spat and touched his tongue. Then looking up to heaven, he sighed and said to him, "Ephphatha," that is, "Be opened." And immediately his ears were opened, his tongue was released, and he spoke plainly.

MARK 7:32–35

Reflection: In this high-tech, digital age, we have great difficulty hearing and discerning the many voices that want our attention. Some of us actually like to be distracted and pulled in many directions because we do not want to hear about the real problems and challenges of life.

As Christians, we can grow spiritually deaf to God, to one another, and to the world around us when we no longer recognize the voice of Christ in the cries of the poor and suffering and lack the courage to speak the gospel message of love and peace. Our preoccupation with the things of the world dulls our senses, making us spiritually deaf and mute.

Like the deaf man, we need to encounter Jesus in the Word of God and be healed by the love of God. When we make the Word of God the centerpiece of our lives, we become more like Christ for others and are able to remain steadfast in doing the work of God in the world.

When we push aside worldly distractions and make time to listen to the voice of God, we open ourselves to become God's messengers of compassion and peace to all who are spiritually deaf.

Ponder: What distracts me from my relationship with God?

Prayer: Lord, your love makes me whole. Open my ears to hear your voice amid all the noise and confusion of life.

Practice: Today I will give my undivided attention in my conversation with others.

Saturday of the Fifth Week in Ordinary Time

YEAR I
Genesis 3:9–24
Psalm 90:2, 3–4abc, 5–6, 12–13

YEAR II
1 Kings 12:26–32; 13:33–34
Psalm 106:6–7ab, 19–20, 21–22

YEARS I AND II
Mark 8:1–10

[Jesus] asked them, "How many loaves do you have?" They said, "Seven." Then he ordered the crowd to sit down on the ground; and he took the seven loaves, and after giving thanks he broke them and gave them to his disciples to distribute; and they distributed them to the crowd.

MARK 8:5–6

Reflection: There is always enough with God. There is always enough love, laughter, joy, peace, forgiveness, and compassion. If we believe that, if we know in our hearts that God is our source for all that is good and life-giving, then we will come to believe that with God, there is always enough food, clothing, shelter, employment, and money for everyone.

Our daily challenge is to bring what we have to God and ask God to transform it into enough. We may worry that we cannot possibly meet all of our responsibilities with the small amount of energy and time at our disposal. We may fear that we do not have the intelligence or talent to handle the tasks facing us. We may be overwhelmed by continued unemployment or financial obligations that are too difficult to meet. Yet we need to keep in mind that God is our source for everything. We need to bring whatever we have to God and ask God to make it enough.

Sometimes God points us to human agencies that can provide us with food or clothing or money for the electric bill. Sometimes God shows us how to deal with an employer who isn't paying us what we are worth. Sometimes God opens our eyes to see that we already have enough and could share a little with someone else.

Ponder: Am I ever completely happy and satisfied with my life?

Prayer: Lord, you bear such great love for your people. Teach me humility and wisdom that I may always put my trust in your compassion and guidance.

Practice: Today I will live in deep gratitude for my life.

Sixth Sunday in Ordinary Time

YEAR A

Sirach 15:15–20
Psalm 119:1–2, 4–5, 17–18, 33–34
1 Corinthians 2:6–10
Matthew 5:17–37 or 5:20–22a, 27–28, 33–34a, 37

> "So when you are offering your gift at the altar, if you remember that your brother or sister has something against you, leave your gift there before the altar and go; first be reconciled to your brother or sister, and then come and offer your gift."
>
> **MATTHEW 5:23–24**

Reflection: There are some experiences in life we'd like to forget. We remember something we did that was hurtful to a family member, a colleague, a friend, or a neighbor. We hope the hurtful things we did in the past will go away, but we are haunted by memories, forced to relive these experiences in our minds. We know we will never have peace in our hearts until we find the courage to say "I'm sorry" to those we have hurt.

There is a voice in our hearts—the voice of God—that calls us to be good, to love others, to make peace, but we ignore this voice and walk in another direction. We choose instead to hold on to the anger because it gives us a sense of power and control. The anger becomes like a virus; it infects us deeply, destroying our lives and interpersonal relationships.

With the grace of God, we can change. Only love can cure an angry heart and heal a wounded soul.

Jesus calls us to be reconciled with those we have hurt along life's journey. We cannot give true worship to God until we make peace with our brothers and sisters. Perhaps we cannot mend all of these relationships, but we must do what we can to make peace with anyone who was the recipient of a harsh remark, a hurtful action, or the silent treatment. When there is less anger and resentment in our lives, there is more love to be shared in the world.

Ponder: Who have I hurt during my lifetime?

Prayer: Lord, you reveal the mercy of God in the world. Forgive me for the times I've hurt others out of anger and resentment.

Practice: Today I will say "I'm sorry" to anyone I may have hurt.

YEAR B

Leviticus 13:1–2, 44–46
Psalm 32:1–2, 5, 11
1 Corinthians 10:31—11:1
Mark 1:40–45

A leper came to [Jesus] begging him, and kneeling he said to him, "If you choose, you can make me clean." Moved with pity, Jesus stretched out his hand and touched him, and said to him, "I do choose. Be made clean!" Immediately the leprosy left him, and he was made clean.

MARK 1:40–42

Reflection: A person with leprosy was considered unclean and banned from participating in the Jewish liturgical life. Because ritual uncleanness was considered contagious, people with this skin disease were isolated from society to keep those who were clean separated from those who were unclean.

In today's world, a person's race, language, color, ethnic background, culture, tribe, gender, sexual orientation, religious tradition, socioeconomic condition, politics, mental and physical capabilities are often used to determine "insiders" and "outsiders." All kinds of barriers are being created to make some people feel superior and others inferior.

We have all been part of a system—a way of

thinking and behaving—that defined who the "lepers" were. As long as such systems continue to exist in our world, there will always be someone who is "clean" or "unclean." When people are separated and isolated from one another, there will be increased poverty, misery, hatred, conflicts, war, and violence.

Jesus is not afraid to share the love and compassion of God with the diseased person. By sharing the love and compassion of God, Jesus dismantles the ritual barrier and restores the person's human dignity. The man with leprosy is reunited with the community.

We need to be more aware of the ways in which we create barriers and discriminate against people. We are given dignity as children of God. Jesus clearly shows us that our work on Earth is to embrace all people and show them the love and compassion of God.

Ponder: Who are the people I keep out of my life?

Prayer: Lord, your love transcends the boundaries of the human condition. Open my eyes to see your face in all people.

Practice: Today I will not avoid people.

YEAR C

Jeremiah 17:5–8
Psalm 1:1–2, 3, 4 and 6
1 Corinthians 15:12, 16–20
Luke 6:17, 20–26

Then [Jesus] looked up at his disciples and said: "Blessed are you who are poor, for yours is the kingdom of God. Blessed are you who are hungry now, for you will be filled."

LUKE 6:20–21

Reflection: Many people in our society are materially poor. They are poor because they are unemployed or underemployed. They lack the financial means to support their families; they are without health insurance; their children cannot go to college; they are discouraged and depressed.

Other people in the world are poor because of natural disasters, political and economic instability, ongoing conflict and violence, widespread famine and drought. These conditions bring about more human despair and death.

Many people in the world are spiritually poor. They have everything they need to live a decent life, but they lack spiritual roots and a sense of purpose. Their hearts are void of happiness, joy, and inner peace. They keep searching for personal satisfaction in all the wrong places.

Whether people are materially poor or spiritually poor, they need the blessed assurance that they have not been abandoned. Those who are materially poor need to know that others are willing to advocate for their needs and make personal sacrifices to support them. Those who are spiritually poor need to recognize that material possessions do not guarantee a life of happiness and peace. The spiritually poor must unburden themselves from their possessions and seek a relationship with God.

So much in our lives and in this world is out of balance because of material and spiritual hunger. Jesus invites all of us to trust in the goodness of God and in the goodness of humanity to satisfy our hungers. We have been created to love one another, to care for one another, and to share our blessings with our brothers and sisters.

Ponder: What are my spiritual needs?

Prayer: Lord, you never forget us; you answer all our needs. Keep me from being anxious about many things.

Practice: Today I will cling less and trust more.

Monday of the Sixth Week in Ordinary Time

YEAR I

Genesis 4:1–15, 25
Psalm 50:1 and 8, 16bc–17, 20–21

YEAR II

James 1:1–11
Psalm 119:67, 68, 71, 72, 75, 76

YEARS I AND II

Mark 8:11–13

[Jesus] sighed deeply in his spirit and said, "Why does this generation ask for a sign? Truly I tell you, no sign will be given to this generation."

MARK 8:12

Reflection: A big house, multiple cars, expensive vacations, and designer jeans are all signs we might interpret to mean success. Hurricanes, tornadoes, tsunamis, and falling asteroids are all signs we might interpret to mean that God is unhappy with the world and is punishing us. The tabernacle, holy water, palms, and incense are all signs we rely on to reassure ourselves that God is really in our midst. Yet Jesus tells us we don't need outward signs to prove the reality of God's love and presence. Jesus points us to God's Spirit within us as our guide to wholeness and union with God.

Deep in our spirit we find peace, serenity, and a vast space empty of distraction, worry, and ambition. Deep in our spirit we face the truth of our status as beloved of God. We face the truth of our strengths and weaknesses. We face the truth of our power to love, heal, and be healed. We face the truth of the entwining of our spirit with God and the glory of our dependence on this God relationship.

Deep in our spirit we know God. We know God loves us. We know God cares about us. We know God understands us.

When we dare to get quiet and sit in stillness with our spirit, we will no longer seek outward signs of God's miraculous goodness. We will be the living sign of God's love and joy in the world.

Ponder: When have I recognized signs of God in my life?

Prayer: Lord, you bear such enormous love for all your people. Teach me your way of love and peace that I may be a sign of joy and compassion for all those I meet.

Practice: Today I will sit alone in a quiet space for ten minutes.

Tuesday of the Sixth Week in Ordinary Time

YEAR I
Genesis 6:5–8; 7:1–5, 10
Psalm 29:1a and 2, 3ac–4; 3b and 9c–10

YEAR II
James 1:12–18
Psalm 94:12–13a, 14–15, 18–19

YEARS I AND II
Mark 8:14–21

> [Jesus] cautioned them, saying, "Watch out—beware of the yeast of the Pharisees and the yeast of Herod."
>
> **MARK 8:15**

Reflection: Yeast is a fungus that reproduces rapidly in the right environment. Some yeast can be used in the baking of bread. Other yeast causes infections. Again, Jesus chooses an example from everyday life to help us discern the path of love and compassion.

When we look at our patterns of behavior, our habits, our word choices, our mood swings, our attitudes, our relationships—what kind of environment do we see? Do we see an environment in which kindness and respect are growing? Do we see an environment in which courtesy and reverence are multiplying? Do we see an environment in which compassion and encouragement are reproducing? Do we see an environment in which peace and harmony are increasing? Do we see an environment in which joy and serenity are developing? Do we see an environment in which acceptance and justice are burgeoning? Do we see an environment in which love is proliferating?

We have the power to create a personal environment that reflects our desire to be like Jesus. We have the power to choose how we speak, how we spend our time, and how we interact with others to reflect the goodness and love of God. We have the power to help the poor, speak out on behalf of those being treated unjustly, and reach out to those who are lonely and discouraged.

Jesus asks us to create a personal environment in which the yeast of peace and hope, of faith and justice, and of love and compassion will grow, multiply, and spread into the lives of others.

Ponder: What kind of yeast am I becoming?

Prayer: Lord, you bless us with your peace and teach us your way of love. Show me how to create an environment in which love and kindness grow and multiply.

Practice: Today I will live in an environment of gratitude.

Wednesday of the Sixth Week in Ordinary Time

YEAR I
Genesis 8:6–13, 20–22
Psalm 116:12–13, 14–15, 18–19

YEAR II
James 1:19–27
Psalm 15:2–3a, 3bc–4ab, 5

YEARS I AND II
Mark 8:22–26

[Jesus] took the blind man by the hand and led him out of the village; and when he had put saliva on his eyes and laid his hands on him, he asked him, "Can you see anything?"

MARK 8:23

Reflection: Jesus himself tenderly holds the man's hand to help him on the way out of the village. Jesus himself puts healing saliva on the man's eyes. Jesus himself lays gentle hands on the man. Jesus shows us that God has a personal interest in each of us. God is always paying attention to our needs, always reaching out to lead us in tenderness and compassion, always touching our lives with gentle healing.

Personal attention is a gift that flows out of those who intentionally follow and imitate Jesus. We have felt the blessing of God's attention to our needs, desires, and wounds. We have felt the grace of God's guidance, comfort, and love. We have learned to be humble in our relationship with God: we know we need God to teach us the way of healing, peace, and love. We have sought time with God to see ourselves and our situations more clearly. We have worked hard and sincerely to change the habits and behaviors that inhibit us from loving ourselves and others.

In gratitude for our intimate knowledge of God's personal care for us, we reach out to touch the lives of those in need. We offer a comforting hand to the grieving, the lonely, and the ill. We walk in compassion with those suffering from discouragement and depression. We see more and more clearly the face of God in those we meet every day.

Ponder: When have I felt God's care and compassion?

Prayer: Lord, you lead me out of the darkness of selfishness into the light of compassion. Help me to bring a touch of encouragement and hope to those in need.

Practice: Today I will offer full and respectful attention to all who communicate with me.

Thursday of the Sixth Week in Ordinary Time

YEAR I

Genesis 9:1–13
Psalm 102:16–18, 19–21, 29 and 22–23

YEAR II

James 2:1–9
Psalm 34:2–3, 4–5, 6–7

YEARS I AND II

Mark 8:27–33

[Jesus] asked them, "But who do you say that I am?"

MARK 8:29

Reflection: When Jesus asks us who we say he is, he is looking for more than a label: God, the Christ, the Messiah, my Lord, friend, healer, companion. Jesus is asking us to step into the mystery of the divine, to open our hearts to the impossibly possible, and to hear the silence of God's voice. Jesus is asking us to let go of our limiting beliefs and embrace the potential of who we are in relationship to God. Jesus is asking us to experience rather than define God and to bring that experience into our everyday lives, our homes, our workplaces, our communities, our relationships.

Prayer and meditation help us to experience God more intimately. Prayer takes many forms: public prayer, speaking from our heart, walking in nature, reading sacred Scripture, and journaling. Prayer is our offering to God. We bring ourselves just as we are and do our best to express to God our love, our longings, and our needs. We examine our strengths and weaknesses and share them honestly with God. We admit our failures to love ourselves and our neighbors, celebrate our successes in shining the light of love and goodness in our corner of the world, and thank God for the many blessings we receive daily.

Meditation is where we let go, quiet our minds, and let the silence of God fill our beings and direct our lives. Meditation is our unique private time with God.

There is no right way to pray or meditate, but we do need to intentionally take the time to pray and meditate so that we may come to experience and know who God is.

Ponder: Who do I say Jesus is?

Prayer: Lord, you hear the cries of all who call to you. Help me to deepen my awareness of your presence and come to know you more intimately.

Practice: Today I will reveal who Christ is by my actions.

Friday of the Sixth Week in Ordinary Time

YEAR I
Genesis 11:1–9
Psalm 33:10–11, 12–13, 14–15

YEAR II
James 2:14–24, 26
Psalm 112:1–2, 3–4, 5–6

YEARS I AND II
Mark 8:34—9:1

[Jesus] called the crowd with his disciples, and said to them, "If any want to become my followers, let them deny themselves and take up their cross and follow me."

MARK 8:34

Reflection: Jesus is not telling us to deny the reality of our circumstances. He is not telling us to deprive ourselves of the pleasures life has to offer. He is not telling us to hide our light or conceal our gifts and talents. Jesus is telling us to put aside our need to be the center of attention and in control of life events. Instead, we need to keep God in the center and be guided by God.

When we let go of the need to be in control, we give God permission to show us what to do each day—and we trust what God shows us. When we let go of our grip on others, on events and situations, we give God the freedom to work in us to provide new solutions and creative outcomes—and we find the courage to act on them. When we let go of our attachment to others, to possessions, to opinions, we give God access to our mind, heart, and soul—and find ourselves viewing life and the people in it with more compassion and less frustration.

When we let go of the need to be in control, we acknowledge that God is in control—and that we need God. We cannot handle the struggles, sorrows, injustices, rejections, illnesses, tragedies, and other human burdens that transpire during our lifetime without God's help. We cannot follow where Jesus leads without God's forgiveness, compassion, and loving guidance to show us the way.

Ponder: When do I feel controlled by others?

Prayer: Lord, you are gracious, merciful, and just. Help me remember that you are in charge. Give me the faith to turn my life over to your loving care.

Practice: Today I will refrain from offering unsolicited advice.

Saturday of the Sixth Week in Ordinary Time

YEAR I
Hebrews 11:1–7
Psalm 145:2–3, 4–5, 10–11

YEAR II
James 3:1–10
Psalm 12:2–3, 4–5, 7–8

YEARS I AND II
Mark 9:2–13

Six days later, Jesus took with him Peter and James and John, and led them up a high mountain apart, by themselves. And he was transfigured before them, and his clothes became dazzling white, such as no one on earth could bleach them.

MARK 9:2–3

Reflection: We need mentors to help us grow and mature. Our parents are our first mentors. They teach us the basics, such as personal cleanliness, social behavior, personal responsibility, study habits, and religious practice. Later we rely on others to help us discern our purpose. We come to discover our calling or vocation in life and look for people to guide us along the way. As we pursue our goals and dreams, we are transformed by the journey, because along the way we are learning new things about ourselves in relationship to the world and the people we encounter.

We need a spiritual mentor to guide us in our search for communion with God. Jesus is the mentor and guide who leads us to God. He teaches us that the journey to God is not easy. The pathway is a rugged challenge that transforms our minds and hearts. If we desire to live in communion with God, we must be willing to detach from the things of the world and surrender our life to Jesus.

Our calling is to be with God. The Word of God is our guide. Without the Word of God we lose our way along the rugged terrain of life. When we feel like we are climbing up the rough side of a mountain, we must remember we are not alone. As we climb the mountains of life, our hope is to be transformed by the light of God's love and peace.

Ponder: What mountain am I climbing at the moment?

Prayer: Lord, you lead and guide me along the way. Increase my faith and trust in you.

Practice: Today I will take a walk in nature and reflect on my relationship with God.

Seventh Sunday in Ordinary Time

YEAR A

Leviticus 19:1–2, 17–18
Psalm 103:1–2, 3–4, 8, 10, 12–13
1 Corinthians 3:16–23
Matthew 5:38–48

"You have heard that it was said, 'You shall love your neighbor and hate your enemy.' But I say to you, Love your enemies and pray for those who persecute you."

MATTHEW 5:43–44

Reflection: What would life be like without an enemy? What would the world look like if there were no more enemies to hate, control, fight against, imprison, or kill? The media is always creating and presenting to us an individual or a group of people to be regarded as the enemy.

Throughout life we encounter people who hurt and disrespect us. Those who mistreat us become our enemies. We withhold our love from them. The enemy can be parents who neglected to care for their children; an alcoholic who emotionally and physically abused a member of the family; a teacher who favored one student over another; a clergy person who betrayed the trust of the people; an employer who refused to pay a just wage; a law-enforcement officer who used excessive force; a colleague who spread vicious rumors; a person who made a racist or sexist remark.

We are not naturally inclined to show goodness and love toward our enemies. Jesus invites us to look within our hearts, to change the way we think and feel about our enemies. We waste so much time and energy harboring hatred toward our enemies. God's Word challenges us not to limit our love to our friends, but to expand our love to include the people who have caused great pain in our lives.

Christians are commanded to love and not hate. The cycle of hatred and violence cannot be broken until we see the enemy as one of our neighbors. Peace and reconciliation are actualized when we allow God's love to triumph over the hatred that keeps us apart.

Ponder: Who are my private and public enemies?

Prayer: Lord, you command me to love my neighbor. May your love dispel the hatred and resentment in my heart so that I may love all people unconditionally.

Practice: Today I will pray for my enemies.

YEAR B

Isaiah 43:18–19, 21–22, 24b–25
Psalm 41:2–3, 4–5, 13–14
2 Corinthians 1:18–22
Mark 2:1–12

"But so that you may know that the Son of Man has authority on earth to forgive sins"—[Jesus] said to the paralytic—"I say to you, stand up, take your mat and go to your home." And he stood up, and immediately took the mat and went out before all of them; so that they were all amazed and glorified God, saying, "We have never seen anything like this!"

MARK 2:10–12

Reflection: When Jesus taught and preached, his words touched the hearts of the people. His words addressed their human condition, their suffering and pain. His words had power and authority because he lived what he preached.

In the gospel passage, Jesus shows us how God intervenes in the paralyzing situations of life and restores the dignity of those who have been diminished by mental, emotional, spiritual, and physical pain beyond their control.

Our children are paralyzed when they are rejected and bullied by others. Husbands and wives are paralyzed when they don't have enough income to provide for their families. The elderly and sick are often paralyzed by loneliness. The poor remain paralyzed because of the lack of food, clean water, and safe shelter. Christians are paralyzed when they neglect to pray and meditate on the Word of God.

In sharing God's Word of love, compassion, and forgiveness, Jesus freed people from the paralyzing conditions of life and restored them to mental, emotional, spiritual, and physical health. As Christians we are called to trust and share with others the power of the Word of God.

Jesus reminds us that every paralyzing situation we experience is an opportunity for the healing power of God's Word. It is in the unexpected, paralyzing situations that we must listen more attentively to the Word of God, discern its meaning in our lives, and trust that all will be well.

Ponder: What is paralyzing me from moving forward in my life?

Prayer: Lord, your Word gives me hope and new life. Help me remember to turn to you when I am paralyzed by fear.

Practice: Today I will face my fear.

YEAR C

1 Samuel 26:2, 7–9, 12–13, 22–23
Psalm 103:1–2, 3–4, 8, 10, 12–13
1 Corinthians 15:45–49
Luke 6:27–38

"Do not judge, and you will not be judged; do not condemn, and you will not be condemned. Forgive, and you will be forgiven; give, and it will be given to you. A good measure, pressed down, shaken together, running over, will be put into your lap; for the measure you give will be the measure you get back."

LUKE 6:37–38

Reflection: We are all guilty of judging others. In judging others, we make ourselves superior to them. We begin to treat them with disdain and disrespect. We are all guilty of condemning others. We condemn people because they don't fit into our way of thinking; they don't wear the right clothing; they did not receive an Ivy League education; they don't speak our language; they don't belong to our culture, race, or nationality; they don't subscribe to our ideology or political party; they don't share in our religious tradition; they are not the right gender or they have a different sexual orientation. When we judge and condemn others, we continue to feed the destructive forces of conflict, division, racism, hatred, war, and violence that tear apart humanity.

When we judge and condemn others, we mock the truth that all people are created in the image and likeness of God and live with dignity as children of God. Jesus offers his followers a countercultural message and an alternate way of life for the common good of all people. Jesus challenges us to be like God: to love and respect all people. As God is generous in love, compassion, and forgiveness, so we, too, must be generous in showing love, compassion, and forgiveness to others.

The pathway to lasting peace and justice for all people begins when we stop judging and condemning people on the basis of their race, skin color, nationality, culture, religious tradition, economic condition, and way of life.

Ponder: Who have I condemned and judged?

Prayer: Lord, your love is beyond measure. Open my heart to show impartial love to all people.

Practice: Today I will not judge or condemn others.

Monday of the Seventh Week in Ordinary Time

YEAR I
Sirach 1:1–10
Psalm 93:1ab, 1cd–2, 5

YEAR II
James 3:13–18
Psalm 19:8, 9, 10, 15

YEARS I AND II
Mark 9:14–29

When [Jesus] had entered the house, his disciples asked him privately, "Why could we not cast it out?" He said to them, "This kind can come out only through prayer."

MARK 9:28–29

Reflection: Some would say greed and selfishness are great demons that need to be cast out of the world. We know the face of individual and corporate greed and how it distorts the human person and undermines the common good of the people.

Greed is the cause of much of the poverty we see in the world. Poverty diminishes the dignity of the human person; it creates oppressive situations and leads people to a state of despair. Selfishness is one of the root causes of moral blindness. Selfishness makes it impossible for people to see the poor and respond to their needs.

In the face of excessive greed and selfishness, we cannot remain indifferent and silent. Motivated by the Word of God, the Christian community can cast out the demons of greed and selfishness by prayer and fasting. There is power in prayer, especially communal prayer. In prayer, we ask God to dismantle the systemic greed crippling the progress of people and the development of communities all over the world. In prayer, we ask God to transform selfish hearts into generous, self-giving hearts.

In addition to prayer, we can fast from apathy and fear and advocate for a more compassionate and just way of life so that the poor and needy can live with dignity. Our fasting fosters a simple lifestyle that reflects a more prudent use of our material resources. We can cast out the demons of greed and selfishness with the nonviolent practices of prayer and fasting.

Ponder: How can I simplify my lifestyle?

Prayer: Lord, you protect the weak and powerless. Free me from the demons of greed and selfishness so that I may respond to the needs of the poor.

Practice: Today I will fast from one meal and donate to the poor.

Tuesday of the Seventh Week in Ordinary Time

YEAR I
Sirach 2:1–11
Psalm 37:3–4, 18–19, 27–28, 39–40

YEAR II
James 4:1–10
Psalm 55:7–8, 9–10a, 10b–11a, 23

YEARS I AND II
Mark 9:30–37

[Jesus] was teaching his disciples, saying to them, "The Son of Man is to be betrayed into human hands, and they will kill him, and three days after being killed, he will rise again." But they did not understand what he was saying and were afraid to ask him.

MARK 9:31–32

Reflection: We have all had ordeals to anticipate: a surgical operation, an intervention for a family member, an appearance in divorce court, a foreclosure on our home. If we are fortunate, we are able to verbalize our worries to people we trust and who will listen without judgment. We find relief in expressing our fears and are able to face our ordeals, knowing that others love and support us.

Anticipating the ordeal of being tried and executed as an insurgent must have caused Jesus a lot of mental and emotional stress. He tells his disciples what's going to happen to him. From all we know about Jesus, he was an approachable person, quick to respond to a cry for help, ready to reach out a helping hand to those in need. Yet the gospel tells us that the disciples are afraid to ask him to clarify his words. Perhaps they were afraid for themselves. If Jesus is to be killed, what will happen to them?

Sometimes we need to let other people have center stage. We need to put our emotions, our stress, and our worries on hold and give others our undivided attention. We need to be generous enough to offer space, time, and kindness so that others can sort out their feelings and confide their problems in us and trust that we will listen with nonjudgmental compassion.

Ponder: How do I respond to others' worries?

Prayer: Lord, you invite us to throw our cares on you. Teach me to listen with my ears and heart to those who are worried and anxious.

Practice: Today I will practice listening to others without trying to fix their problems.

Wednesday of the Seventh Week in Ordinary Time

YEAR I
Sirach 4:11–19
Psalm 119:165, 168, 171, 172, 174, 175

YEAR II
James 4:13–17
Psalm 49:2–3, 6–7, 8–10, 11

YEARS I AND II
Mark 9:38–40

But Jesus said, "Do not stop him; for no one who does a deed of power in my name will be able soon afterwards to speak evil of me. Whoever is not against us is for us. For truly I tell you, whoever gives you a cup of water to drink because you bear the name of Christ will by no means lose the reward."

MARK 9:39–41

Reflection: Being named the Most Valuable Player is an honor. Those who receive this award are part of an elite group of athletes. Being listed in Forbes Top 100 is a prestigious recognition. Those listed are part of a unique club of wealthy people. Winning the Nobel Peace Prize is one of the highest honors bestowed on a person who has championed the cause of peace, justice, and reconciliation between people. Those who receive this award belong to a very distinct inner circle.

Organizations throughout the world have strict rules and guidelines for membership. The purpose of these rules and guidelines is to let certain people in and keep others out. Being part of an elite group makes some people feel superior to others; it gives them a sense of power and prestige.

Being a member of the Christian community is not like being a member of an elite club. We are called to be humble persons, eager to serve the needs of others. We are expected to follow the example of Jesus who came to serve and not be served. We must be aware that God's love and power is given to all people to be used for good. As humble servants, we must show compassion to all and work for peace.

Ponder: When do I feel superior to others?

Prayer: Lord, you are the humble servant of God. Teach me to be humble and to serve all people with a generous heart.

Practice: Today I will try not to be the center of attention.

Thursday of the Seventh Week in Ordinary Time

YEAR I
Sirach 5:1–8
Psalm 1:1–2, 3, 4 and 6

YEAR II
James 5:1–6
Psalm 49:14–15ab, 15cd–16, 17–18, 19–20

YEARS I AND II
Mark 9:41–50

[Jesus said] **"If any of you put a stumbling block before one of these little ones who believe in me, it would be better for you if a great millstone were hung around your neck and you were thrown into the sea."**

MARK 9:42

Reflection: Our mission as followers of Jesus is to build God's kingdom of love and joy with our attitudes, words, and actions. Our mission is to offer everyone we meet the respect and compassion they deserve as children of God. Our mission is to reach out to offer a hand or to grab a hand so that no one stumbles over the sorrow, tragedy, illness, discouragement, or despair that life events can bring.

Sometimes we sabotage our mission. Sometimes

we make a joke at someone else's expense, spread a little gossip, or betray a confidence. Sometimes we speak sarcastically, sigh impatiently, or roll our eyes in disgust. Sometimes we manipulate others' feelings, talk others into doing something laden with risk, or treat people of different races and cultures with disrespect. Sometimes we blame others for our problems, criticize others unjustly, or refuse to take responsibility for ourselves.

When we become aware of our human failings and the harm we cause or have caused others, we feel a heavy weight in our spirit. We know we have been a stumbling block for others. We know we have undermined others' joy, trust, and sense of self-worth.

We don't have to carry that millstone of guilt. We can begin right now to make changes so that our words, attitudes, and actions reflect our commitment to walk with Jesus and build up the kingdom of hope, peace, compassion, and love.

Ponder: What attitudes and behaviors of mine are stumbling blocks for others?

Prayer: Lord, your mercy is great. Forgive my shortcomings and failures. Take away all that makes me a stumbling block for those who seek your love and peace.

Practice: Today I will speak kindly and encouragingly to all those I encounter.

Friday of the Seventh Week in Ordinary Time

YEAR I
Sirach 6:5–17
Psalm 119:12, 16, 18, 27, 34, 35

YEAR II
James 5:9–12
Psalm 103:1–2, 3–4, 8–9, 11–12

YEARS I AND II
Mark 10:1–12

[Jesus] left that place and went to the region of Judea and beyond the Jordan. And crowds again gathered around him; and, as was his custom, he again taught them.

MARK 10:1

Reflection: We all have customs we practice, whether we are conscious or unconscious of them. We may have the custom of celebrating holidays with family and friends. We may have the custom of paying our respects to a grieving family by attending a wake or funeral. We may have the custom of sitting down for a family dinner every night. We may have the custom of tucking our children into bed and kissing them good night. We may have the custom of starting or ending our day and our meals with prayer.

Sometimes our customs are not life-giving. We may have the custom of shopping on Sundays. We may have the custom of wasting food. We may have the custom of littering and polluting the environment. We may have the custom of lying when we're afraid. We may have the custom of isolating ourselves when we feel hurt by others. We may have the custom of texting friends instead of talking to them. We may have the custom of overspending and building up debt. We may have the custom of deriding others to cover up our own lack of healthy self-esteem. We may have the custom of criticizing the government without taking any positive action for social reform.

Customs provide a background rhythm out of which we lead our lives. We need to look deeply at our customs to discern if their rhythm is synchronized with that of Jesus, whose custom was to teach the way of love, peace, and compassion.

Ponder: Which of my customs do I need to change?

Prayer: Blessed are you, O Lord. Open my eyes and heart to learn your customs of love, truth, and peace.

Practice: Today I will begin a new custom of thanking God for my life.

Saturday of the Seventh Week in Ordinary Time

YEAR I
Sirach 17:1–15
Psalm 103:13–14, 15–16, 17–18

YEAR II
James 5:13–20
Psalm 141:1–2, 3 and 8

YEARS I AND II
Mark 10:13–16

[Jesus said to them] "Let the little children come to me; do not stop them; for it is to such as these that the kingdom of God belongs."

MARK 10:14

Reflection: Jesus blesses the little children with tender hands and loving embraces. He sees into the hearts and minds of the children and sees their innocence and infinite capacity to love.

Adult hearts are also capable of innocence and an infinite capacity to love. Jesus teaches us that to truly be his followers, we must clear our lives of all that impedes our capacity for innocent wonder and joy in the world's blessings. Jesus teaches us that a heart open to love and trust—like a little child's—is our path to God's kingdom of love and peace. Innocence is the quality of being receptive to God's love in all forms. We look for goodness in others and find it. We notice the natural beauty of our world and rejoice in it. We take pleasure in the accomplishments of others and feel no envy. We welcome others into our lives and have an ever-expanding sphere of influence in the world.

We may have had ugly experiences in our lives; we may have been abused, rejected, or abandoned. Yet the innocence in our hearts allows us to still find goodness in people and in the world. We accept the love of others and are nurtured by it. We love simply, without strings or attachment, without jealousy or judgment.

Innocence leads us to let go of whatever habits we may have developed as protective measures against being hurt by others. Innocence is our deepest knowledge of God's personal love and care for us, our trust in God's loving embrace, healing hands, and blessing.

Ponder: When have I robbed the innocence of others?

Prayer: Lord, your kindness is everlasting. Give me the courage to let go of all that blocks me from dwelling in innocence.

Practice: Today I will treat myself with tenderness.

Eighth Sunday in Ordinary Time

YEAR A

Isaiah 49:14–15
Psalm 62:2–3, 6–7, 8–9
1 Corinthians 4:1–5
Matthew 6:24–34

"No one can serve two masters; for a slave will either hate the one and love the other, or be devoted to the one and despise the other. You cannot serve God and wealth."

MATTHEW 6:24

Reflection: We become what we worship. We become what we give our hearts and attention to. In a sense, we become what we wear, we become what we eat, we become what we drink. We need to be more aware of what we allow to control and consume our lives. We need to discern what is important in life and what we really need to live a good, healthy life versus what we want for the thrill of the moment.

The secular culture tries to convince us that we don't need God in our lives. The servants of the marketplace sell us the idea that the more material things we buy and possess, the happier we will be. The more food and drink we consume, the better we will feel about ourselves. If we want instant gratification, all we have to do is surrender our hearts to the gods of the marketplace.

We cannot live a divided life. We cannot have a Bible in one hand and a credit card in the other. We cannot love and serve both equally. If we seek first to live in accordance with the Word of God, then our life becomes less divided and more balanced.

The Christian life is centered on God, to whom we offer our undivided love. Contrary to the pleasure-seeking messages of the marketplace, the gospel invites us to live from Jesus' perspective of total trust in God. For Christians, authentic life is found in a relationship with God and not in the marketplace.

Ponder: What is my heart's true desire?

Prayer: Lord, you are the source and center of my life. Give me the grace to love you with all my mind, heart, soul, and strength.

Practice: Today I will devote fifteen minutes to prayer and meditation.

YEAR B

Hosea 2:16b, 17b, 21–22
Psalm 103:1–2, 3–4, 8, 10, 12–13
2 Corinthians 3:1b–6
Mark 2:18–22

"No one sews a piece of unshrunk cloth on an old cloak; otherwise, the patch pulls away from it, the new from the old, and a worse tear is made. And no one puts new wine into old wineskins; otherwise, the wine will burst the skins, and the wine is lost, and so are the skins; but one puts new wine into fresh wineskins."

MARK 2:21–22

Reflection: It's all about the image. If we don't have the right image, we will not be accepted; we are outside the mainstream of life. We are more worried about image and less concerned about the substance of things.

Outward appearances do matter; they are usually indicators of an inner reality. They express how we feel about ourselves and life in general. Sometimes the outward appearances hide negative thoughts, old emotional wounds, deep spiritual confusion, and lingering self-doubt.

Being well groomed and well dressed can make us look attractive and desirable, but underneath those things is a poor self-image. Having a lot of money in the bank, a beautiful home, and a luxury car can make us feel happy and successful. Underneath these flamboyant trappings may be a sense of spiritual emptiness. Earning a diploma or a certificate, passing the bar or civil-service exam qualifies us to be a public servant. In practice, they may bring arrogance and abuse of power.

Being a Christian is less about what church we belong to and more about allowing the substance of the gospel to transform our minds and hearts. We can attend church each week, pay our tithe, follow the rules, quote the catechism, and still ignore Jesus' command to love one another. Being Christian means living each day with a heart renewed by the Word of God. We must learn to live with the skin and wine of the gospel: love, compassion, peace, and forgiveness.

Ponder: Do my actions match my words?

Prayer: Lord, you know and accept me as I am. Help me to be faithful to the gospel.

Practice: Today I will let my actions speak louder than my words.

YEAR C

Sirach 27:4–7
Psalm 92:2–3, 13–14, 15–16
1 Corinthians 15:54–58
Luke 6:39–45

"No good tree bears bad fruit, nor again does a bad tree bear good fruit; for each tree is known by its own fruit."

LUKE 6:43–44A

Reflection: Our actions reveal the nature of our hearts and the content of our lives. When our hearts are filled with unconditional love, we have the capacity to show love to all people regardless of their race, language, culture, or way of life. When our hearts are filled with compassion, we have the capacity to reach out to the poor, feed the hungry, clothe the naked, shelter the homeless, visit the sick and the imprisoned, and welcome the stranger. When our hearts are filled with peace, we have the capacity to resolve our differences, avoid conflict, and live a nonviolent life. When our hearts are filled with forgiveness, we have the capacity to experience inner freedom and heal broken relationships.

Because we are made in the image and likeness of God, we have the capacity to be goodness in the world. God has planted in our hearts the seeds of goodness. As we grow and mature, we must learn how to cultivate these seeds and bear good fruit through our actions. When life becomes disordered and unmanageable, it is our responsibility to use our gifts and talents for the common good of all people.

A distinctive Christian character is informed and shaped by the Word of God. The teachings of Jesus found in the gospels help us to realize our capacity for goodness and inspire us to bring forth from our hearts the fruit of love, compassion, peace, and forgiveness. God's nature is in our hearts. People will come to know God by the fruit we bear.

Ponder: What kind of fruit do I bear in the world?

Prayer: Lord, you show me the pathway of goodness and truth. Help me to bear the fruit of love, compassion, and peace.

Practice: Today I will be intentional about doing good deeds for others.

Monday of the Eighth Week in Ordinary Time

YEAR I
Sirach 17:20–24
Psalm 32:1–2, 5, 6, 7

YEAR II
1 Peter 1:3–9
Psalm 111:1–2, 5–6, 9 and 10c

YEARS I AND II
Mark 10:17–27

Jesus, looking at him, loved him and said, "You lack one thing; go, sell what you own, and give the money to the poor, and you will have treasure in heaven; then come, follow me."

MARK 10:21

Reflection: Jesus looks at us and loves us. He sees our lacks, knows our weaknesses, knows we will probably never sell all we own and give the money to the poor. Yet he loves us just as we are.

When we look at others, we tend to notice their lacks and failings. We think we know how they could improve themselves and their lives. We know we could advise them how to be different. We forget to look with love. We forget to love others despite their weaknesses and failings. We forget to let love tell us how to look and what to see.

Every day we have the opportunity to find something to love about the people we meet. When we look at others with the intention of finding something to love, we start seeing with new eyes. We might see insecurity masked by bossiness. We might see self-doubt obscured by irritation and anxiety. We might see a desire to please and a fear of being rejected. The more deeply we look, the more we see a reflection of our own insecurity, self-doubt, and fear. We begin to realize that all people want to be loved, accepted, and understood. We begin to expand our capacity for compassion. We begin to soften our expectations of perfection.

The more we look with love at others, the more we learn to let others be our teachers, the mirrors that reflect God's love.

Ponder: How do I look at myself and others?

Prayer: Lord, you created each of us as a great work of art. Help me look beyond surface irritations to see your love and goodness in others.

Practice: Today I will deliberately look for one thing to love in each person I meet.

Tuesday of the Eighth Week in Ordinary Time

YEAR I
Sirach 35:1–12
Psalm 50:5–6, 7–8, 14 and 23

YEAR II
1 Peter 1:10–16
Psalm 98:1, 2–3ab, 3cd–4

YEARS I AND II
Mark 10:28–31

Jesus said, "Truly I tell you, there is no one who has left house or brothers or sisters or mother or father or children or fields, for my sake and for the sake of the good news, who will not receive a hundredfold now in this age—houses, brothers and sisters, mothers and children, and fields with persecutions— and in the age to come eternal life."

MARK 10:29–30

Reflection: Sometimes the idea of forsaking our obligations, leaving our many responsibilities, and walking away from our family, jobs, and commitments seems like it would bring us great relief. No more pressure. No more stress. No more worry.

Jesus is telling us that we can let go of pressure,

stress, and worry by taking his path of love and peace. Jesus is telling us that we aren't trapped by possessions or by what other people think or do. He is asking us to let go of the fear, doubt, uncertainty, and need to be in control that prevent us from following him. Jesus is asking us to make up our minds to join him on the adventure of loving ourselves and our neighbors—with loving God as our beginning and end and with God's love as our faithful guide.

Sometimes when we choose the path of love and peace, the people in our lives will think we're crazy. They won't be comfortable with our new attitudes and behaviors. They may try to manipulate us to be the way we used to be.

This is what we leave behind. We leave behind our attachment to others' fear, disapproval, and anger and keep following Jesus on the path of healing and wholeness.

Ponder: What do I need to leave behind to follow Jesus?

Prayer: Lord, all the ends of the Earth have seen your salvation. Help me let go of all that prevents me from following your path of love, compassion, and peace.

Practice: Today I will give away one of my possessions.

Wednesday of the Eighth Week in Ordinary Time

YEAR I
Sirach 36:1, 4–5a, 10–17
Psalm 79:8, 9, 11 and 13

YEAR II
1 Peter 1:18–25
Psalm 147:12–13, 14–15, 19–20

YEARS I AND II
Mark 10:32–45

They were on the road, going up to Jerusalem, and Jesus was walking ahead of them; they were amazed, and those who followed were afraid.

MARK 10:32

Reflection: Torture and death await Jesus in Jerusalem, but he's out in front of everyone, leading the way. Jesus has complete confidence in the will of God, even if it doesn't seem to make sense for him to be killed when he is doing so much good in the world. Jesus does not manipulate, connive, or try to control the way in which events are unfolding. He walks in perfect harmony with the moment, trusting that the part he has to play in God's universal plan will eventually make sense.

Sometimes the things we hear God asking us to do don't make sense in the moment. Sometimes we ignore God's voice because we think what we're hearing is irrational. We make ourselves crazy trying to find other solutions. We become stressed, anxious, and irritable.

We need to remember that God's Law is based on faith and love, not logic. We need to remember that God sees the whole picture of our lives, of the world, of all time. We need to trust that what God sees makes sense and that how we lead our lives has importance in God's vision.

When we let go of the rational and trust God, we experience peace of mind and a sense of freedom. We feel centered again. We can take action, confident that God is with us, giving us everything we need in the moment: courage, dignity, wisdom, and serenity. We can walk with Jesus, comfortable with letting God make sense out of human chaos and in harmony with ourselves and the world.

Ponder: When have I trusted God's will for me, even when it didn't make sense?

Prayer: Lord, come to my aid. Help me to trust and follow you, even when my mind argues with my heart.

Practice: Today I will listen to my heart when making decisions.

Thursday of the Eighth Week in Ordinary Time

YEAR I
Sirach 42:15–25
Psalm 33:2–3, 4–5, 6–7, 8–9

YEAR II
1 Peter 2:2–5, 9–12
Psalm 100:2, 3, 4, 5

YEARS I AND II
Mark 10:46–52

Then Jesus said to him, "What do you want me to do for you?"

MARK 10:51

Reflection: Jesus wants to know how he can help Bartimaeus, the man who is blind. He expects Bartimaeus to articulate his wants and needs. He cares about what Bartimaeus wants. And when Bartimaeus says he wants to see, Jesus gives him sight.

Jesus teaches us that God cares about the things we care about. We can go to God with faith that God wants to hear our needs, desires, hopes, and ideas. Our part is to express our desires—and then let them go. We can trust that God has heard us and will respond in God's time.

God hears and responds to others' needs and

wants too. Sometimes we are God's response. Sometimes we are the ones who provide clothing, food, or shelter for those in need. Sometimes we are the ones who listen to someone who needs to talk. Sometimes we are the ones who encourage those who need reassurance. Sometimes we are the ones who visit or call others who need companionship.

Our desire to be like Jesus opens our hearts to respond to the needs of others. As we learn to pay attention to others and their needs, we find ourselves becoming more generous and less grasping. We become more compassionate and less dismissive. We become more patient and less judgmental. Showing others how much we care about them is one way we share our faith and trust in God's care for all people and their needs.

Ponder: What makes it hard for me to ask God for what I want?

Prayer: Lord, you made us and we are yours. Give me the courage to ask you for what I want and need—and the trust to let go after asking.

Practice: Today I will search my heart to discover what I really want and then ask God for it.

Friday of the Eighth Week in Ordinary Time

YEAR I

Sirach 44:1, 9–13
Psalm 149:1b–2, 3–4, 5–6a and 9b

YEAR II

1 Peter 4:7–13
Psalm 96:10, 11–12, 13

YEARS I AND II

Mark 11:11–26

Then they came to Jerusalem. And he entered the temple and began to drive out those who were selling and those who were buying in the temple, and he overturned the tables of the money changers and the seats of those who sold doves.

MARK 11:15

Reflection: Jerusalem, where he will be crucified, is stirring up uncomfortable emotions in Jesus. In the human process of accepting his approaching loss of life, Jesus experiences the same emotions we do as we struggle to accept reality. Feeling anger is one facet of the process, and Jesus uses the power of his anger to rid the Temple of those he calls "thieves."

When we experience loss of any kind—the death

of a loved one, illness, divorce, unemployment—we visit and revisit many emotional states before we finally accept the loss. Our struggle to reach acceptance is often unconscious. We may stuff all our feelings and pretend nothing happened. We may find ourselves yelling at God. We may blame ourselves or somebody else. We may keep busy to avoid facing the loss. We may plunge deeply into dark sadness. Finally—when we are ready and not before—we let go and accept the loss. With acceptance comes a return to consciousness and a sense of peace. We can now admit that we are not in control of life events.

Jesus' actions in Jerusalem reassure us that we walk in solidarity with God when we suffer loss and are grieving. With God at our side, it is safe for us to be aware of the uncomfortable feelings that come with loss. With God at our side, we can learn to release our feelings in ways that help us without harming others.

Ponder: What reality do I need to accept?

Prayer: Lord, your grace touches every facet of my life. Help me to accept reality without fear.

Practice: Today I will be gentle with myself when difficult emotions arise in me.

Saturday of the Eighth Week in Ordinary Time

YEAR I
Sirach 51:12cd–20
Psalm 19:8, 9, 10, 11

YEAR II
Jude 17:20b–25
Psalm 63:2, 3–4, 5–6

YEARS I AND II
Mark 11:27–33

Jesus said to them, "I will ask you one question."

MARK 11:29

Reflection: We need to ask questions to help us grow. Yet we don't have to answer when someone asks us a question. We can be like Jesus and ask a question back. We can try to generate a dialogue rather than feel obliged to satisfy someone's need to know.

The art of dialogue establishes a relationship between people. It is a form of respectful conversation in which ideas are explored, feelings are discerned, viewpoints are aired, and new solutions are offered. It is a time of intimacy, a time of deeper communion, a time of coming to understand others in a different way.

When we dialogue, we allow others to know our minds and hearts more completely. We bring our experience and wisdom to the conversation. We hear what others' experience and wisdom have to teach us. We may not understand all we hear. We may not agree with all we hear. We may not want to hear all that's being said. Yet if we keep our ears, minds, and hearts open, we will always learn something new, something to ponder, something we may ultimately reject, or something we may ultimately incorporate into our own experience.

When we pray, we enter a dialogue with God. We bring our questions to God and listen for answers. Sometimes God's answers are new questions for us to consider. Our God-dialogue is a time of searching our hearts and minds to gain insight into ourselves, to uncover the wisdom that already lies within us, and to be peaceful about not knowing all the answers.

Ponder: What kind of questions do I ask God?

Prayer: Lord, you are wise and trustworthy. Open my mind and heart to your love and guidance that I may grow in kindness and compassion.

Practice: Today I will deliberately open a respectful dialogue with another person.

Ninth Sunday in Ordinary Time

YEAR A

Deuteronomy 11:18, 26–28, 32
Psalm 31:2–3, 3–4, 17, 25
Romans 3:21–25, 28
Matthew 7:21–27

"Everyone then who hears these words of mine and acts on them will be like a wise man who built his house on rock. The rain fell, the floods came, and the winds blew and beat on that house, but it did not fall, because it had been founded on rock."

MATTHEW 7:24–25

Reflection: Building our lives on material things is not the best approach. Our possessions do not guarantee ultimate happiness, security, and peace. No matter what we accumulate, our lives can collapse and be completely ruined by some misfortune.

Our experiences teach us that life is unpredictable and fragile. We are never prepared for the sudden mental, emotional, spiritual, or physical events that disrupt the flow of our lives. Life-altering moments that are beyond our control force us to rethink the meaning and foundation of our lives.

The sudden loss of a loved one can trigger a flood of deep emotional pain. Going through the experience of separation and divorce can bring about a spiritual crisis. Overwhelming stress and anxiety can stir up mental anguish. Living an unhealthy lifestyle can present some physical challenges. In these and similar situations, we realize we need faith and the love of others to sustain us.

The Word of God teaches us that with faith in Jesus, we can withstand the storms and trials of life. Our faith in Jesus helps us to remember that God is with us, walks with us, and saves us when we are being battered by the winds of personal crisis. No matter what we are going through, our faith in Jesus, who is the rock of our life, holds everything together.

Ponder: What is the source and foundation of my life?

Prayer: Lord, you are the source and foundation of my life. Help me remember that you are with me in the storms and trials of life.

Practice: Today I will remain calm when life becomes chaotic.

YEAR B

Deuteronomy 5:12–15
Psalm 81:3–4, 5–6, 6–8, 10–11
2 Corinthians 4:6–11
Mark 2:23—3:6 or 2:23–28

We are afflicted in every way, but not crushed; perplexed, but not driven to despair; persecuted, but not forsaken; struck down, but not destroyed; always carrying in the body the death of Jesus, so that the life of Jesus may also be made visible in our bodies.

2 CORINTHIANS 4:8–10

Reflection: People of faith trust in the power of the death and resurrection of Jesus. They can survive the human condition, knowing that the power of Christ is revealed not through strength, but through weakness. The paradox of the Christian faith is that Christians find their true identity and power in brokenness.

People of faith are afflicted with debilitating diseases, but their spirit is not crushed. They give witness in their bodies to the power of Jesus' resurrection.

People of faith are challenged each day by the secular messages and trends of the culture. They stand in the world as countercultural signs of Jesus' presence, never losing confidence in the power of the gospel to renew and transform the face of the Earth.

Christians are persecuted in all parts of the world. They remain true to God and never waiver in their commitment to live a faithful, fruitful life.

People of faith are killed for advocating for the poor and the oppressed, but their prophetic lives inspire others to carry out the mission of Jesus to lift up the lowly and to set captives free.

We must understand that the Christian life is not easy for those who take the gospel seriously. We must strive with all our mind, heart, soul, and strength to live in the power of the death and resurrection of Jesus. Whatever good we do in the world is accomplished in and through the life of Jesus.

Ponder: When have I found myself in a powerless situation?

Prayer: Lord, your death and resurrection restore my faith, hope, and love in you. Strengthen my resolve to walk through life by faith and not by sight.

Practice: Today I will be careful not to overpower or take advantage of people.

YEAR C

1 Kings 8:41–43
Psalm 117:1, 2
Galatians 1:1–2, 6–10
Luke 7:1–10

I am astonished that you are so quickly deserting the one who called you in the grace of Christ and are turning to a different gospel—not that there is another gospel, but there are some who are confusing you and want to pervert the gospel of Christ.

GALATIANS 1:6–7

Reflection: We are challenged each day by messages contrary to the gospel. The media bombards us with messages of greed and violence. Images in magazines, on the Internet, and on billboards entice us to buy our way to happiness and peace. We are conditioned to think that wealth and power are all that matter in life. We buy into a more subtle message, one that says God is no longer the center of our lives. We believe the lie that we are autonomous, the center and creator of our own world.

We must be careful not to succumb to deceptive messages that attempt to manipulate us. We must not desert the gospel of Christ in favor of a different gospel. We desert the gospel of Christ when we abandon our relationship with God and become self-centered. We confuse the meaning of the gospel of Christ when we refuse to be like God in the world, when we fail to love, forgive, and be reconciled with one another. We pervert the gospel of Christ when we deny the truth that everyone is created in the image of God.

Our life must be shaped by this gospel so that we become messengers of hope and peace to all people. The life, death, and resurrection of Jesus is the foundation of the Christian faith. This is the gospel that moves our hearts to give witness to Christ in a confused, troubled world.

Ponder: How do I distort the gospel of Christ?

Prayer: Lord, your death and resurrection is good news for my life. Help me to trust your good news when I am confused and distracted.

Practice: Today I will not be a hypocrite. I will practice what I preach.

Monday of the Ninth Week in Ordinary Time

YEAR I
Tobit 1:3; 2:1a–8
Psalm 112:1b–2, 3b–4, 5–6

YEAR II
2 Peter 1:2–7
Psalm 91:1–2, 14–15b, 15c–16

YEARS I AND II
Mark 12:1–12

> Then [Jesus] began to speak to them in parables. "A man planted a vineyard, put a fence around it, dug a pit for the wine press, and built a watchtower; then he leased it to tenants and went to another country."
>
> **MARK 12:1**

Reflection: Jesus teaches by telling stories that feature familiar situations for the people of his time. He shares the stories with the people so that they may reflect on them and gain a deeper understanding of God's presence in the world and in people of every kind.

Most of us have a story to share at the end of any given day. We might tell of a funny encounter with a stranger. We might tell of a dismaying report from the doctor. We might tell of something annoying our boss did. We might tell of an exciting opportunity that came our way. We might tell of an embarrassing failure on our part.

We tell our stories as interestingly as possible so that our audience pays close attention. Often we tell our stories to elicit suggestions, congratulations, or commiseration. Sometimes by telling our stories, we clarify for ourselves exactly what the situation meant to us and are able to process the emotional impact of the experience.

When we tell stories from our day, we can go beyond the entertainment or shock value and take the opportunity to look for God's presence in the story. Our stories can be a means of deepening our understanding of how God walks with us every step of our day. Our stories can be a means of teaching others to find God's peace, compassion, and love in ordinary life events.

Ponder: What stories from my life do I share with others?

Prayer: Lord, you are the cornerstone of my life. Help me create life stories that reflect your love, peace, and goodness.

Practice: Today I will share a story from my day that reflects my confidence in God's peace-filled presence.

Tuesday of the Ninth Week in Ordinary Time

YEAR I
Tobit 2:9–14
Psalm 112:1–2, 7–8, 9

YEAR II
2 Peter 3:12–15a, 17–18
Psalm 90:2, 3–4, 10, 14 and 16

YEARS I AND II
Mark 12:13–17

Jesus said to them, "Give to the emperor the things that are the emperor's, and to God the things that are God's."

MARK 12:17

Reflection: Faith, hope, peace. Love, compassion, joy. Trust, forgiveness, justice. Mercy, kindness, gratitude. Gentleness, patience, forbearance. Acceptance, courage, wisdom. Generosity, self-control, goodness. Respect, courtesy, humility. Humor, accountability, honesty. Awareness, commitment, detachment. Freedom, intimacy, serenity. Wonder, service, sharing. Integrity, maturity, unity.

These are things that belong to God.

We give God the things that are God's by giving them to the people we meet every day. Although our desire to become more like God inspires us to practice the things of God, we are not always patient, loving, and kind. We know we need practice to become patience, become love, become kindness in the world. When we fail, we can give our failure to God too. We learn humility from our failures. We learn to trust God's guidance more. We learn to find the courage to continue practicing.

Every day is a chance to give the things of God to God. We can find humor in the unexpected. We can detach from others' negativity. We can be accountable for our actions. We can speak respectfully to our family and friends. We can exercise self-control when we feel angry. We can experience the wonder of God's creation in nature and in the beautiful mystery of each person we encounter. We can speak out in defense of someone who is being treated unjustly. We can serve those who are in need.

Giving God the things that are God's is our calling. We are called to be godlike, to be a living reminder of God's presence in the world, and to show the world the way of peace and love.

Ponder: What things of God do I give to others?

Prayer: Lord, fill me with your kindness and love that I may give a glimpse of you to the world.

Practice: Today I will intentionally practice a God quality.

Wednesday of the Ninth Week in Ordinary Time

YEAR I
Tobit 3:1–11a, 16–17a
Psalm 25:2–3, 4–5ab, 6 and 7bc, 8–9

YEAR II
2 Timothy 1:1–3, 6–12
Psalm 123:1b–2ab, 2cdef

YEARS I AND II
Mark 12:18–27

Jesus said to them, "Is not this the reason you are wrong, that you know neither the scriptures nor the power of God?"

MARK 12:24

Reflection: We tend to cling to our opinions and to insist we're right. Yet it's so liberating to admit we may be wrong, to let go of rigid thinking and learn to respect others' opinions, and to choose happiness over being right.

Jesus points out that intimate study of the Scriptures opens our minds and hearts to new ways of understanding ourselves and others. Reflecting on God's Word in sacred Scripture gives us insight into God's infinite love, patience, and creative genius.

Prayerful time with the Scriptures shows us the limitations of our human knowledge and reveals the mystery and power of God.

As we read and reflect on the Scriptures, we learn to let go of habitual thinking, stubborn mindsets, and harsh judgment. We learn about God's covenant of love with humankind. We learn about God's love for us, a love more mindful than a mother's for her child. We learn about God's intimate knowledge of us before we were even in the womb.

We learn how to be like God from Jesus, who teaches us the way of peace and reconciliation. Jesus teaches us forgiveness, compassion, and humility. Jesus teaches us to share what we have with the poor, to open our doors to those in need of shelter, to visit those who are lonely, discouraged, ill, or imprisoned.

With the Scriptures as our study guide and the power of God to fill us with courage, we can let go of our opinions and arrogance. We can open ourselves to a life in which love is more important than being right.

Ponder: When was the last time I read and reflected on the Scriptures?

Prayer: Lord, you are the God of the living. Open my mind and heart to your power that I may live and love fully.

Practice: Today I will admit when I am wrong.

Thursday of the Ninth Week in Ordinary Time

YEAR I
Tobit 6:10–11; 7:1bcde, 9–17; 8:4–9a
Psalm 128:1–2, 3, 4–5

YEAR II
2 Timothy 2:8–15
Psalm 25:4–5ab, 8–9, 10 and 14

YEARS I AND II
Mark 12:28–34

Jesus answered, "The first is, 'Hear, O Israel: the Lord our God, the Lord is one; you shall love the Lord your God with all your heart, and with all your soul, and with all your mind, and with all your strength.' The second is this, 'You shall love your neighbor as yourself.' There is no other commandment greater than these."

MARK 12:29–31

Reflection: The universal law is love. Since our daily mission is to practice the law of love, it's a good practice to take the time each evening to look back over our day to see how we have carried out the command to love.

Where did we love during the day? Maybe we ran

an errand for someone. Maybe we listened carefully when someone needed to talk. Maybe we recycled papers and cans. Maybe we refrained from littering. Maybe we helped out at home without being asked. Maybe we defended someone who was being bullied. Maybe we exercised self-control when we felt angry, annoyed, or impatient.

Where did we fail to love during the day? Maybe we told ourselves we were stupid, ugly, or lazy. Maybe we spoke sarcastically to someone. Maybe we walked by someone without a greeting. Maybe we were rude to our family. Maybe we made fun of someone less capable. Maybe we made a racial slur. Maybe we lied.

Any time we act contrary to Jesus' model of forgiveness, compassion, and acceptance, we have failed to show love. Any time we show forgiveness, compassion, and acceptance, we are keeping the law of love and acting in harmony with God. Cultivating a practice of awareness of the moment allows us to start over at any moment and choose the way of love.

Ponder: When have I loved and failed to love?

Prayer: Lord, your way is love. Teach me to love others even when it's difficult.

Practice: Today I will check in with myself to see if I am loving or failing to love.

Friday of the Ninth Week in Ordinary Time

YEAR I
Tobit 11:5–17
Psalm 146:1b–2, 6c–7, 8–9a, 9bc–10

YEAR II
2 Timothy 3:10–17
Psalm 119:157, 160, 161, 165, 166, 168

YEARS I AND II
Mark 12:35–37

And the large crowd was listening to [Jesus] with delight.

MARK 12:37

Reflection: Jesus is always here to teach us. The Scriptures guide us and refresh our knowledge of Jesus' mission in the world. By our baptism, we have been named priest, prophet, and king as one with Jesus and have the graced freedom to fearlessly seek the Spirit's guidance in understanding the teachings of Jesus. By our baptism, we have the moral obligation to ensure that God's command to love be the first consideration in our daily lives.

Sometimes we forget we have the ability to discern the meaning of the Scriptures. Sometimes we ignore the gift of our personal relationship with

God. Sometimes we are afraid of being misunderstood by others when we share our thoughts, opinions, and feelings on the Scriptures. Sometimes we refuse to be open to another point of view about the Scriptures. Sometimes we are more focused on the letter of the law rather than the spirit of the law. Sometimes we close our hearts to what is revealed by God in the Scriptures.

We need to approach the Scriptures with a sense of awe, delight, and reverence. We can trust that the Spirit will open our minds to the knowledge and truth that Jesus is God's anointed one. We can trust that the Spirit will teach us to listen attentively to the Word of God in the Scriptures. We can trust that the Spirit will open our ears to hear God's voice of peace, compassion, and love. We can trust that the Spirit will inspire us to pray, empower us to proclaim the gospel, and move us to serve the needs of others with compassion.

Ponder: When have I been moved and inspired by God's Word?

Prayer: Lord, your Word brings love, peace, and delight to my life. Give me the grace to be love, peace, and delight for others.

Practice: Today I will discern the voice of God in my life.

Saturday of the Ninth Week in Ordinary Time

YEAR I

Tobit 12:1, 5–15, 20
Tobit 13:2, 6efgh, 7, 8

YEAR II

2 Timothy 4:1–8
Psalm 71:8–9, 14–15ab, 16–17, 22

YEARS I AND II

Mark 12:38–44

[Jesus] sat down opposite the treasury, and watched the crowd putting money into the treasury. Many rich people put in large sums. A poor widow came and put in two small copper coins, which are worth a penny.

MARK 12:41–42

Reflection: Jesus takes time to observe the people and what they are doing. He sees the poor widow give all she had. Jesus shares his observation with his disciples, offering them a new teaching to reflect on.

It takes awareness to observe what goes on around us. It takes a caring heart to understand what motivates us. It takes detachment to observe ourselves and others without negative judgment. It takes love to turn our observations into spiritual reflections that will deepen our knowledge of our own limitations and of God's infinite goodness.

The gift of consciousness, of moment-to-moment awareness, is a precious one. We can learn to cultivate this gift by practicing the art of observing without judgment. Starting by watching our breath go in and out, we become aware of the vastness of the moment. We become aware of the deep stillness within us, the presence of God within. We become aware of the Spirit who gives life to each breath. We become aware of our dependence on God, of our intricate, intimate bond with God the creator.

Awareness brings responsibility. We cannot be aware of the Spirit within us without acknowledging the Spirit within each of God's children. We can no longer ignore poverty, injustice, or prejudice. We can no longer dismiss the needs of those less fortunate.

Our awareness renews Jesus' teaching: the teaching of love, compassion, and the joy of loving our neighbor as our self.

Ponder: How aware am I of the present moment?

Prayer: Lord, you teach us to love our neighbor as ourselves. Open my eyes to see and respond to the needs of the poor.

Practice: Today I will be aware of how I speak and act toward others.

Feast Days

Solemnity of the Most Holy Trinity

YEAR A

Exodus 34:4b–6, 8–9
Daniel 3:52, 53, 54, 55
2 Corinthians 13:11–13
John 3:16–18

The grace of the Lord Jesus Christ, the love of God, and the communion of the Holy Spirit be with all of you.

2 Corinthians 13:13

Reflection: We carry within us the genetic makeup of our parents passed on to us at birth. We have within us some of their features, facial makeup, intelligence, gifts and talents, behaviors. We share things in common with the members of our family because we are connected to a family tree.

The Holy Trinity is the DNA of the Christian life. We have been imprinted with the divine life and love of the Triune God. We have within our nature the instinct of the Trinity: the instinct to love, share peace, create family, and live in communion with others. We do not reflect often enough on our divine origin, yet we need to pay attention to this God instinct within us and use our creative imagination to fashion our lives in the likeness of the Triune God.

In these challenging times, when people are divided against one another because of race, language, culture, tribe, nationality, and religious belief, it is important to remember that we come from the community of God where there is eternal unity, peace, and love. God has given us everything we need to bring about unity, peace, and love in the world.

As Christians, we have a unique calling and obligation to resemble the life of the Trinity in the world. This means making an effort to align our thoughts with the wisdom of God, to form our hearts with the love of Jesus, and to unite our souls with the Spirit of God. Our mission in life is to carry out the Trinity's mission of bringing together all people into one human family.

Ponder: What does my life look like in the Trinity?

Prayer: Lord, you live in communion with God and the Holy Spirit. Help me to live in communion and peace with all people.

Practice: Today I will strive to be in harmony with everyone I encounter.

YEAR B

Deuteronomy 4:32–34, 39–40
Psalm 33:4–5, 6, 9, 18–19, 20, 22
Romans 8:14–17
Matthew 28:16–20

"Go therefore and make disciples of all nations, baptizing them in the name of the Father and of the Son and of the Holy Spirit, and teaching them to obey everything that I have commanded you. And remember, I am with you always, to the end of the age."

MATTHEW 28:19–20

Reflection: Wherever we go, the Triune God is with us. If we remember this truth as we journey through life, we can be more faithful witnesses to the gift of love that comes forth from the Trinity.

In the life of the Triune God there is no division, no conflict, no tension, no violence, no war, and no inequality. When we reflect deeply on the inner nature of the Trinity, we begin to see our own nature and the mission that has been entrusted to us. Our life is with the Triune God. We must do our best to live in the world from within the community of God. When we are grounded in this reality, our life and relationships will begin to resemble the inner life of the Trinity.

Strengthened by the grace of God, we are capable

of doing what Jesus has commanded us to do: to love one another as God has loved us. We are collaborators with the Trinity. We have been entrusted with the mission of building up the kingdom of God on Earth by bringing people into the life of the Trinity.

People will know that God is with us when we inspire them to love all people, to serve the poor, and to uphold the sanctity of life. As Christians, we have been commissioned to do our part to share our faith in God, to teach and live as Jesus did, and to live in peace and communion with all people.

Ponder: What has God commissioned me to do with my life?

Prayer: Lord, you command me to love all people. Remove the prejudice that keeps me from loving my brothers and sisters.

Practice: Today I will spend time with someone I have neglected.

YEAR C

Proverbs 8:22–31
Psalm 8:4–5, 6–7, 8–9
Romans 5:1–5
John 16:12–15

"All that the Father has is mine. For this reason I said that he will take what is mine and declare it to you."

JOHN 16:15

Reflection: There can be no true act of love, no pure gift of self if we are holding something back. True love always involves self-sacrifice. The Triune God is always caught up in the act of total love and pure self-sacrifice.

God holds nothing back. All that God possesses is poured out to us and for us in Jesus. There is no selfishness to be found in God; there is only self-giving. Everything we need to live a good life is found in God's gift of self in Jesus. Our faith in Jesus gives us access to the gifts of God: unconditional love, compassion, and peace.

Our life in God means a life of self-giving, a life for others, and a life of humble service. In the gospels, Jesus reveals the vision of the kingdom of God. Through Jesus, God shows us how to live an authentic human life. Through Jesus, God tells us unambiguously to love one another, forgive one another, and be reconciled with our brothers and sisters.

Through Jesus, God urges us to look beyond ourselves, beyond our own needs, and to take care of the poor in our midst. Through Jesus, God opens a way for us to experience a bit of eternity on earth.

The fundamental message of God in and through Jesus is one of selfless love. God's will is that we share generously what we have and not withhold the gifts of love, compassion, peace, and forgiveness from anyone. God teaches us through the life of Jesus that anything that diminishes the life and dignity of the human person is contrary to the wisdom of God.

Ponder: What am I holding back from others?

Prayer: Lord, you willingly gave up your life for the salvation of the world. Give me the courage to love freely and unconditionally.

Practice: Today I will pray for the members of my family and tell them I love them.

Solemnity of the Most Holy Body and Blood of Christ

YEAR A

Deuteronomy 8:2–3, 14b–16a
Psalm 147:12–13, 14–15, 19–20
1 Corinthians 10:16–17
John 6:51–58

Because there is one bread, we who are many are one body, for we all partake of the one bread.

1 CORINTHIANS 10:17

Reflection: What is a home without a table? The table is where family members gather to give thanks to God for the many blessings of life, to eat a meal together, to share old and new stories, to ponder the deep questions of life, and to simply enjoy one another's presence. The table creates bonds of love and friendship and community. When we eat and drink together around a table, we willingly participate in the drama of the human condition.

What is the church without a table? The table is where we gather to give praise and thanks to the Triune God, through whom all things were made. We gather to listen to the Word of God and to ponder its meaning in our lives. We come together as the people of God to participate in the drama of the unfolding of God's love revealed in the breaking of the one bread and the drinking of the one cup. We come together in the Eucharist to express our common faith in the death and resurrection of Jesus as the source and foundation of the Christian life.

We must see the connection between the table in our homes and the table in the church. When we bring the family gathered at home to gather around the table of the Lord, we allow ourselves to be transformed into the body of Christ. Like Christ, we must share what we have received by going forth into the world to preach the gospel and serve the needs of all.

Ponder: How often do I share a meal with my family? How often do I participate in the Eucharist?

Prayer: Lord, through your Body and Blood you offer me the gift of eternal life. Help me to make sacrifices and share what I have with the poor.

Practice: Today I will invite friends and family to eat together.

YEAR B

Exodus 24:3–8
Psalm 116:12–13, 15–16, 17–18
Hebrews 9:11–15
Mark 14:12–16, 22–26

While they were eating, he took a loaf of bread, and after blessing it he broke it, gave it to them, and said, "Take; this is my body." Then he took a cup, and after giving thanks he gave it to them, and all of them drank from it. He said to them, "This is my blood of the covenant, which is poured out for many."

MARK 14:22–24

Reflection: The Eucharist teaches us some important lessons for living in the world. When we gather around the table of the Lord, we learn how to live and act like Jesus. In the Eucharist, Jesus teaches us that life is a blessing. No matter what we experience, all is a blessing, and we need to give thanks to God.

Jesus shows us in his own life that brokenness is an essential aspect of the Christian life. Unless we are broken, we cannot share in and understand the human condition. When we experience the pain of brokenness, we are made vulnerable and are united with the suffering of others. When we recognize that we share in the common weakness of the human condition, we are more likely to pour out love and compassion.

At the heart of the Eucharist is the act of self-giving. The actions of Jesus found in the Eucharist must become our way of acting in the world. The Eucharist becomes a way of life, a countercultural sign against selfishness, greed, the abuse of power, and violence. All who are united in the Eucharist are called to give to others what they have received through the sacrifice of Christ: the love, compassion, and peace of God.

Ponder: Why am I afraid to be vulnerable?

Prayer: Lord, out of brokenness and weakness you saved my life. Help me to embrace my weakness so that I can walk in solidarity with the poor and suffering.

Practice: Today I will be more sensitive to the pain and suffering of the people around me.

YEAR C

Genesis 14:18–20
Psalm 110:1, 2, 3, 4
1 Corinthians 11:23–26
Luke 9:11b–17

And taking the five loaves and the two fish, he looked up to heaven, and blessed and broke them, and gave them to the disciples to set before the crowd. And all ate and were filled. What was left over was gathered up, twelve baskets of broken pieces.

LUKE 9:16–17

Reflection: We live in a "super-sized" culture where we have more than we need. We are accustomed to eating out and often do not consume all the food we order. Perhaps we bring the leftovers home for another meal, but generally they are thrown into the garbage bin. So much food gets wasted while so many people in the world starve to death.

The Eucharist is not just about feeding our spiritual hunger; it is also a call to feed those who lack food and water. We cannot eat at the table of the Lord and not think about our moral duty to feed the poor. We must be aware that we become the body of Christ by our participation in the Eucharist. We receive from the Eucharist our common mission to feed the hungry, to share with them the love and compassion of God.

The Eucharist challenges us to reassess our lifestyle—especially our food consumption—in light of God's generosity. We need to be more mindful of the ways we waste food and abuse the resources of the Earth. In the Eucharist we are called to give to others what Jesus has given to us: food for life. Jesus, who is present with us in the Eucharist, invites us to be more proactive in our efforts to eradicate global poverty.

Ponder: How much food do I waste during the week?

Prayer: Lord, you love me and answer all my needs. Help me to be less self-focused in life and more attentive to the needs of others.

Practice: Today I will be mindful of what I eat and not be wasteful. I will tithe and give to a local charity.